An Everyday MIRACLE

What is humanly impossible is possible for God - Luke 18:27

JENNIFER MUSZIK

AN EVERYDAY MIRACLE
WHAT IS HUMANLY IMPOSSIBLE IS POSSIBLE FOR GOD - LUKE 18:27

Copyright © 2015 Jenn Muszik.

Editor – Kylie George

All rights reserved. No part of this book may be used or reproduced by any means, graphic, electronic, or mechanical, including photocopying, recording, taping or by any information storage retrieval system without the written permission of the author except in the case of brief quotations embodied in critical articles and reviews.

iUniverse books may be ordered through booksellers or by contacting:

iUniverse
1663 Liberty Drive
Bloomington, IN 47403
www.iuniverse.com
1-800-Authors (1-800-288-4677)

Because of the dynamic nature of the Internet, any web addresses or links contained in this book may have changed since publication and may no longer be valid. The views expressed in this work are solely those of the author and do not necessarily reflect the views of the publisher, and the publisher hereby disclaims any responsibility for them.

Any people depicted in stock imagery provided by Thinkstock are models, and such images are being used for illustrative purposes only. Certain stock imagery © Thinkstock.

ISBN: 978-1-4917-8115-9 (sc)
ISBN: 978-1-4917-8116-6 (hc)
ISBN: 978-1-4917-8114-2 (e)

Library of Congress Control Number: 2015919330

Print information available on the last page.

iUniverse rev. date: 12/11/2015

Contents

Introduction vii
Chapter 1: Our Beginning 1
Chapter 2: What is Happening? 8
Chapter 3: Needing to Breathe 15
Chapter 4: This Can't be the End! 18
Chapter 5: Everyone Near and Far, "Please Pray!" 29
Chapter 6: Holding Our Breath 39
Chapter 7: What Do I Say to our Kids? 43
Chapter 8: Keeping Our Focus on God and His Miracles 51
Chapter 9: Keeping It Real 60
Chapter 10: Reality Setting In 69
Chapter 11: Hold It Together – No Time for a Breakdown! 79
Chapter 12: Two Steps Forward...One Step Back – It's Still Progress 86
Chapter 13: Filling My Soul and Praying for Paul's 96
Chapter 14: Praise the Lord! Paul is Awake! 106
Chapter 15: Awake ≠ Aware 114
Chapter 16: No Time for Sleep 118
Chapter 17: Moving Day – When One Door Closes ... 123
Chapter 18: Tomorrow is Never Guaranteed – A Commitment to Our Marriage 130
Chapter 19: Let's Get Moving – A Commitment to Building Strength 135
Chapter 20: This is God's Story 143
Chapter 21: This is a Process – Be Patient 152
Chapter 22: One Step at a Time 157
Chapter 23: Time for a Visit with our Little Ones 164
Chapter 24: A Healing Body and Swirling Mind 169
Chapter 25: From Frustration to Focus – God's Got This! 175
Chapter 26: What??? I'm Not Ready!!! 185

Chapter 27: Back at Home – Finding Balance and a New Routine 192
Chapter 28: God is Good – ALWAYS! 204
Chapter 29: Coming Full Circle 212
Chapter 30: Our "New" Normal 219
Chapter 31: Holy Week – Deepening Our Relationship with Christ 223
Chapter 32: Hallelujah & Amen! Praise God for all of Paul's Progress! 228
Chapter 33: What about Me? Where is God Guiding My Next Step? 232
Chapter 34: God's Perfect Plan 238
Afterward 245
Appendix
    Song List: 249

Introduction

It was in 2009 when I told my husband, Paul, I wanted to write a book. I remember him looking at me and asking, *"What would you write it about?"* The question was both supportive and sarcastic at the same time. Paul is quick-witted, quite funny and also amazingly supportive of me! But, the question gave me pause. My response was something like, *"Well, I'm not sure, but I feel like this is something I am meant to do."*

In 2013, after some personal struggles with fertility, I started a blog – God's Fertile Ground. I thought, *this must be my outlet.* I wasn't supposed to write a book, I was just supposed to *write*.

When I started the blog, I wanted to go back to my early childhood and specifically look for times when God showed up in my life. While I knew He was always there, I also knew there were times when I felt closer to Him and other times when I didn't. My desire was to look back and see how God showed up in the past, so that I could be more aware of how He was showing up in the present.

Blogging helped to fulfill both my desire to write – and my desire to more clearly see God's Work in my life. I was able to see the ways He helped guide and direct my life...when I let Him.

Something else I learned during this journey was God's desire for a relationship with each and every one of us. He wanted a relationship with me. He was always there. He knew me before anyone else. He stitched me in my mother's womb. He calls me by name. He had done so very much to develop a relationship with me. What had I done to develop a relationship with Him?

The blog presented an opportunity to dig deeper into His Word. I spent more time in The Bible, reading His Word and listening to His Story. I started to see both how He was working in my life and in the lives of others. The more I pursued getting to know Him, the closer I felt to Him and the easier it was for me to see Him in both the big and the everyday things.

So, there it was. I was supposed to write, I was supposed to deepen my relationship with Christ, and I was supposed to share it with others.

I remember listening to Pastor Andy Stanley talk about the difference between "good things" and "God things." As I recall, he differentiated the two something like this: Good things sound good at the moment, but given time and circumstances, the glow of the opportunity fades. God things sound good, and continue coming back. That doesn't mean that God things need to happen right now, it just means that God has put His Vision of our work into us, and He will help us to identify when the time is right to act.

While there had been fairly large events in our lives where we could clearly see God's Hand working miracles for us, none of them seemed *book-worthy*. That all changed in February 2015, when God clearly saved Paul from what everyone thought was certain death.

It was time. This was a God thing.
And, God was telling me it was time to start.

Before jumping right into that story, I wanted to share two different passages from the Gospel of Matthew. These passages helped me both come up with a title for the book and gave me the courage to actually write out this story.

The first passage is about Jesus performing the miracle of multiplication.

Jesus Feeds a Great Crowd (Matthew 14:13-21, GNB)

"When Jesus heard the news about John, he left there in a boat and went to a lonely place by himself. The people heard about it, so they left their towns and followed him by land. Jesus got out of the boat, and when he saw the large crowd, his heart was filled with pity for them, and he healed those who were ill.

That evening his disciples came to him and said, "It is already very late, and this is a lonely place. Send the people away and let them go to the villages to buy food for themselves."

"They don't have to leave," answered Jesus. "You yourselves give them something to eat!"

"All we have here are five loaves and two fish," they replied.

"Then bring them here to me," Jesus said. He ordered the people to sit down on the grass; then he took the five loaves and the two fish, looked up to heaven, and gave thanks to God. He broke the loaves and gave them to his disciples, and the disciples gave them to the people.

Everyone ate and had enough. Then the disciples took up twelve baskets full of what was left over. The number of men who ate was about 5,000, not counting the women and children.

Jesus performed a miracle – the miracle of multiplication. He took five loaves and two fish to feed over 5,000.

Let's first stop here. What seemed impossible – feeding over 5,000 with two fish and five loaves, was clearly possible for Jesus. To Him, this was just another _Everyday Miracle_ He was providing. He was clearly showing His disciples that, with God, nothing is impossible!

There is a second part of this story that is often missed. He had the disciples collect the remnants, had them physically pick up the remaining parts. He had them collect the miracle. They now could share their experience of watching Jesus take five loaves and two fish, feed a crowd of over 5,000, and still have twelve baskets of remnants left over.

They had seen Jesus perform other miracles – making the blind see, the lame walk, the dead come alive. This was another *Everyday Miracle* He was performing. But this time, He had them physically collect it; pick it up with their own hands. I cannot imagine how that activity strengthened their faith. I cannot imagine how it might have impacted their desire and ability to share God's Work. How it may have increased their passion as they shared this story.

This was one reason why I wanted to write this book for those of you who witnessed the *Everyday Miracle* that God provided in the saving and healing of Paul. You were with us each step of the journey through the blog or Facebook. You were praying along side us. You were collecting the miracles God provided – each breath, each tiny improvement.

I want you to have it. I want you to collect it. I hope having this, as a reminder, will increase your passion and excitement as you share God's *Everyday Miracle* of healing Paul.

This brings me to the second Gospel passage, broken down into two parts. This passage gave me the courage to write the story and share it with more than just those who witnessed God's *Everyday Miracle* alongside us.

The Parable of the Sower (Matthew 13:1-9, GNB)
"That same day Jesus left the house and went to the lakeside, where he sat down to teach. The crowd that gathered around him was so large that he got into a boat and sat in it, while the

crowd stood on the shore. He used parables to tell them many things.

"Once there was a man who went out to sow corn. As he scattered the seed in the field, some of it fell along the path, and the birds came and ate it up. Some of it fell on rocky ground, where there was little soil. The seeds soon sprouted, because the soil wasn't deep. But when the sun came up, it burnt the young plants; and because the roots had not grown deep enough, the plants soon dried up. Some of the seed fell among thorn bushes, which grew up and choked the plants. But some seeds fell in good soil, and the plants produced corn; some produced 100 grains, others sixty, and others thirty."

And Jesus concluded, "Listen, then, if you have ears!"

Jesus Explains the Parable of the Sower (Matthew 13:18-23, GNB)

"Listen, then, and learn what the parable of the sower means. Those who hear the message about the Kingdom but do not understand it are like the seeds that fell along the path. The Evil One comes and snatches away what was sown in them. The seeds that fell on rocky ground stand for those who receive the message gladly as soon as they hear it. But it does not sink deep into them, and they don't last long. So when trouble or persecution comes because of the message, they give up at once. The seeds that fell among thorn bushes stand for those who hear the message; but the worries about this life and the love for riches choke the message, and they don't bear fruit. And the seeds sown in the good soil stand for those who hear the message and understand it: they bear fruit, some as much as 100, others sixty, and others thirty."

I share this passage because I have been each of these:

- I have been The Path. I have listened. I have known the words to say. But, I didn't truly understand what they meant. They were in my head, but not in my heart.
- I have been the Rocky Ground. I would listen to the message, and I would feel good that there was a God watching over me. But, the message didn't last long.
- I have been the Thorn Bush. I have listened to the message and followed for some time. But, when what God wanted me to do would conflict with what I wanted to do, I would quickly JUMP OFF the path and make my own choices.
- I have been the Good, Fertile Soil. More often now, I find myself here. I seek a relationship with Jesus by reading the Bible, listening to Christian pastors and Christian music. I pray continually and seek God's guidance in decisions big and small. And, I try to share this with others.

My prayer for this book is that it helps anyone reading it both collect this miracle that God has provided and sparks a desire for a deeper relationship with Jesus. I received so many messages from people who were with us on this journey speaking of how this has caused them to pray deeper and more boldly than ever before.

This is a story of our ever-living, all-powerful and ever-loving God! He moved mountains, He parted seas, and He provided many miracles in the healing of my husband. So, this isn't our story – this is His story.

My prayer is that this book helps you to collect and share in one of God's *Everyday Miracles.*

Chapter 1: Our Beginning

June 2014: Our Family, Paul & I, Paulie 6, Noah 4, Sarah 2

I truly think we live in Mayberry, USA! I mean, seriously. This picture was taken in late June 2014 at the front of our subdivision. We live in a beautiful neighborhood with amazing neighbors who might as well be family, in an excellent school system, near all the amenities you could ever want. We are truly blessed to be here, and we know it as we have had the opportunity to move five times in our marriage. While the other locations were really good, they just cannot compare to our current neighborhood – as it has it all! We try not to take it for granted. We try to raise our children with a sense of balance. We want them to know how lucky they are to live such a life of privilege (my politically correct word for spoiled). As this story unfolds, you will see many examples of why I wanted to share this from the beginning.

Friday, February 13, 2015
Our next-door neighbors, who are great examples of those as close to us as family, had moved about 3 ½ hours away in January for a career opportunity. While we were excited for their opportunity, we knew we would miss them terribly! So, we planned a visit in February to celebrate both our friend's birthday & Valentine's Day with each other. Plus, our favorite cover band was playing at a local restaurant, so it promised to be a fun-filled weekend!

As our former neighbors arrived, I was finishing up a phone call with a colleague from my work. We were waiting to hear information on the fate of our team as our company was going through a reorganization and we knew our positions had the potential to be eliminated. She had heard that the report would be done soon, and the likelihood of our team continuing did not look good. Let's just say the car ride to the restaurant was filled with lots of conversation about this potential change, but the minute we walked in the door, we left that behind. Another couple from the neighborhood joined us, and the six of us had a great time listening to the band, dancing, eating and celebrating together!

Saturday, February 14, 2015 – Happy Valentine's Day!
The next morning, my husband, Paul, got up before 6:00am and went to his usual Saturday morning basketball game with other men from the area. He had been playing basketball 4-5 times per week the previous several months...well, maybe almost a year. We had taken some time off the summer prior as we were dealing with my diagnosis of cervical cancer. We had caught it early, and we had learned there was a great chance for cure with a hysterectomy. While this was a scary diagnosis, we were thankful that it was caught early. And, while others might

be focused on the loss of the potential for additional children, we had given that decision to God the year prior.

See, it took us over 2 years to get pregnant with our first son, Paulie. We lost a pregnancy between Paulie and our second son, Noah. Then, we were blessed to conceive fairly quickly with our daughter, Sarah. And then experienced another lost pregnancy. So, I consider myself a mother of five, three on Earth and two in Heaven.

After the loss of our second pregnancy, we had given the decision for more children to God – well, it was always His decision, but we were more conscious of it. If it was His Will for us to have additional children, then His Will be done. If not, we were okay with it. That said, I would often pray for a sign or an answer to the question. While I was okay with either answer, I really wanted to know the answer.

After getting the diagnosis, I remember standing in the shower thinking back to all of those prayers for an answer. Here it was, right in front of me, an answer to my prayers. The decision was clear. We were going to move forward with the hysterectomy, cure the cancer, and know that we were meant to be a family of three on Earth and two in Heaven.

We went through the surgery and healing process at the end of 2014.

 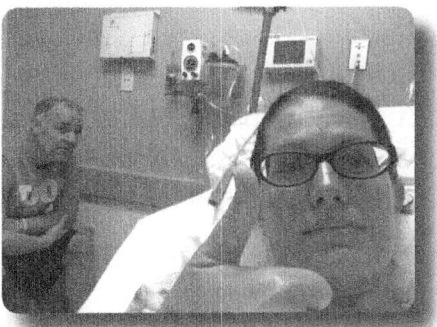

September 30, 2014: Here are photos of Paul and I, in the waiting room and the pre-op room, before the procedure. You see my "thumbs up" indicating that we are good, God's got this!

I cannot stress enough how wonderful our family, friends and neighbors are. A great friend and neighbor started a meal train (http://www.mealtrain.com) for us. This is an amazing way for people to help others in need by providing food for their families. We were so very thankful for this service. During my recovery, we had food nearly every day for a month! We also had many people stop by to ensure Paul had everything he needed, make trips to the grocery, help with our three kids, etc. Just some examples of how amazing our family, friends and neighbors are – we are truly blessed!

As I was healing, Paul started back into his basketball routine. Plus, we both needed to diet due to all the great food we had been eating!! Paul and I were dedicated to encouraging each other to live a healthier lifestyle, for us and for our kids. We were eating better and increasing our activity. I was spending more time on the treadmill; thanks to the plastic contraption Paul bought me for Christmas that held my laptop when I walked. Paul was back to basketball, walking, and starting weight training. He had also started a weight loss competition with some high school friends as he had gotten back up to 260lbs at the end of the year...on a 6' frame – that was truly not healthy.

So, Paul got up and went to basketball that morning. When he came home, he mentioned his back hurt. When he lifted up his shirt, there was a red mark on his back – about 2-3 inches high and 5-6 inches wide. It looked like someone had slapped him in the back. While he knew it hurt, it was Valentine's Day, and our friends were in town. We had plans to go out to a local steakhouse for our Valentine's Day dinner. Plus, we all assumed the pain would go away soon.

Sunday, February 15, 2015

Paul woke up and jumped in the shower. The mark on his back was still there and it was still hurting. I noticed the mark seemed to be just above a spot on his back where we had previously tried to pop what we thought was a pimple (sorry for anyone who is grossed out by this!). We had both tried to squeeze the "pimple" a few times, but it never popped.

We decided if it still hurt on Monday, we would go to the doctor.

That evening, I had to leave for a meeting at my college sorority around 7:00pm. While it had been sixteen years since I graduated, I was thankful for the opportunity to stay engaged as an advisor to the chapter.

When I returned around 9:00pm, Paul was already in bed, complaining of fever, sweats and chills. We knew he needed to go to the doctor the next day, and I would likely be canceling my trip to New York that week for work.

> **Background:**
> *I had been working for a pharmaceutical company for over sixteen years. I had the opportunity to hold eight different positions during those years, hence the reason why we had moved five times in our marriage. When we found out we were pregnant, after more than two years of trying, we truly wanted one of us to stay home with our child (and hopefully more in the future). Paul and I agreed that he would stay home and I would pursue furthering my career. While this wasn't an easy choice, it was the best one for our family.*
>
> *When this situation with Paul occurred, I was working in a virtual role – meaning, while we didn't have to move for my job, I did need to travel to our NY headquarters several times per month. That next week was one I was planning to be in NY.*
>
> *Based on Paul's current condition, it didn't look like that was going to happen.*

Monday, February 16, 2015 – President's Day

As soon as we woke up, we called the doctor's office. Paul's usual provider was out of the office that day, but there was another doctor who could either see him right away or at

2:00pm. Since Paul wanted me to go with him and our youngest two children were still sleeping, we decided on the 2:00pm time slot. Throughout the day, Paul's pain got progressively worse, so he was not very happy that we made that decision. He truly wished we had gone earlier, hoping that he would have received medicine to take this pain away.

At 2:00pm, we were at the doctor's office and the nurse was asking lots of questions since the office had just changed it's electronic health record system. After she entered the information into the system, she took a look at Paul's back. She had mentioned the potential for this being shingles, and went to get the doctor.

When the doctor came into the room, he asked Paul a few additional questions. He looked at the mark and made notes in the computer. He stated he also believed this was shingles, so he wasn't going to do a flu or strep test. While I thought there might be value in doing the additional tests, the doctor seemed very confident in the diagnosis, so I didn't question it.

He prescribed medicines to help with the shingles and told Paul that he would likely be in pain for another few days. After that, he should be feeling better.

We left the office, filled the prescriptions at the pharmacy, and went home. I proceeded to e-mail my team leader and tell him that I needed to work from home that week. Paul was in a lot of pain and not able to take care of the kids. I needed to be home for him, and for them.

Tuesday & Wednesday, February 17-18, 2015

The next two days, Paul was definitely feeling pretty bad. His body was still achy and he continued to fluctuate between chills and sweats. One new symptom that started was uncontrollable hiccups. The hiccups sounded like they were coming up from his toes. They were loud and would shake his entire body. We weren't sure why they were starting, but thought it might be due to Paul's lack of appetite. He hadn't been eating much and had been taking the medicine he was prescribed. Again, we thought this would go away sometime soon.

The daytime seemed to be better for him than nighttime. During the day, he was able to rest on the couch or nap on the recliner. At night, he would try to sleep in bed, but he couldn't get comfortable because he was in a lot of pain. That said, we thought this was normal with the diagnosis of shingles per the doctor's discussion.

As we were getting ready for bed that Wednesday night, Paul knew I was supposed to be at an all-day meeting at Butler the next day. I was working on having others cover the work, but he said that he wanted me to go. Paul was used to taking care of all the "inside of the house" work so I could go to my "outside of the house" work. He didn't want to be a burden. He thought he was feeling better and wanted me to get back to my normal routine. I said I would see how he felt the next morning.

Chapter 2: What is Happening?

Thursday, February 19, 2015

When I got up that morning, Paul said he thought he was feeling better. My meeting at Butler had been delayed due to the weather, so I decided I would drive Paulie (our oldest son) to school. I had the time, and it was very cold and windy. Plus, it was always fun to spend extra time with him in the morning!

After dropping Paulie off at school, I called Paul to check-in since he was still pretty sleepy when I left. I wanted to see how he was feeling and if he was okay with my going to my meeting. He said that I should go. While he wasn't feeling 100% yet, he was feeling better. So, I went, but told him that my phone was with me and I would come back for anything he needed.

When I got to Butler, I was talking with the women about Paul. And, it is hard to admit now, but at the time I said, "It is just shingles and it has been three days. He needs to get over it."

Please know, there are no excuses for that statement. I was going off of the doctor's comment that Paul should be feeling better by now. And, Paul and I handle illnesses differently. I am more of a "power through" kind of a girl where he is more of a "give me medicine and take care of me" kind of a guy. So, I assumed that he should be feeling better by now.

But, at 12:45pm when my phone rang and I received the following texts, I knew something was wrong:

Paul:
I think Im dizzy from lack of calories.
Which meds at 1
Violent throw up right after I tried to eat and took my lunch…need you
Took my pills

                                                                  Me:
                                                                 On my way

---

I also received a call from Paul's mom. She was on FaceTime with Paul when he showed her how the rash had spread, which he didn't notice until that morning. The red, sunburn-like rash from his back had appeared under his arms and between his legs. She also heard his violent throw up as he described in his text and they were both scared.

When I called Paul, he sounded normal – sick, but normal. He described his rash to me, so I told him I would call the doctor on my way home. When I called the doctor's office, I spoke with someone there and told her what was happening. She said it was probably a reaction to the steroids given to him for the shingles. She said to stop at the pharmacy for some Benadryl and stop the steroids for the afternoon. We were to call if things didn't get better or got worse.

I arrived home from the pharmacy just before 2:00pm and saw Paul's rash.

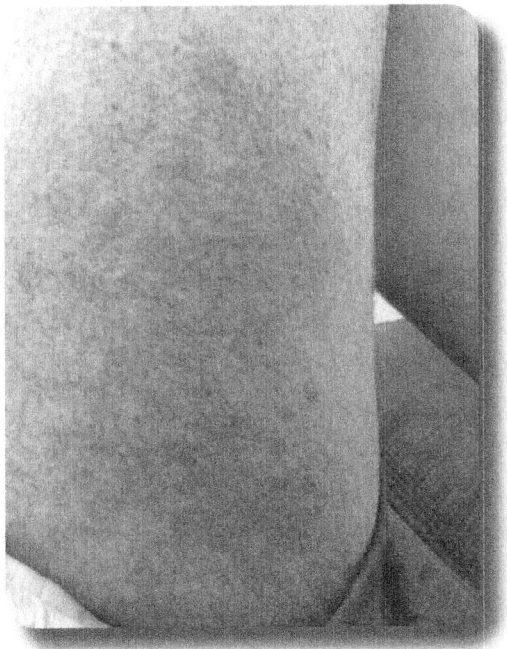

Here is the visual of the rash on his leg. You can start to see some of the darker purplish color at the bottom of his shorts.

Seeing this, I knew I needed to take Paul back to the doctor. I put Noah and Sarah (our itty bittys) into the car and went back in to get Paul. At this time, he was pretty weak and I could tell he was scared by what he was seeing and how he was feeling.

On the way to the doctor's office, I called to see if we could get an appointment with the provider who saw Paul on Monday. We were told he couldn't see us, and we would need to go to the Immediate Care side of the office. Truly, that was fine with me; Paul just needed to be seen.

I dropped Paul off at the door and parked the car. It took him a long time to get into the office. When I walked in with our itty bittys a few moments later, Paul was really out of breath and could barely stand up straight. The Immediate Care doctor was able to see him right away.

Upon seeing Paul, he asked the doctor who saw Paul on Monday to come into the room - *immediately.* Both seemed very concerned and called for an ambulance. They were going to get him admitted to the hospital. At that time, I still didn't know what was wrong. I was assuming he needed a couple of days of major antibiotics & steroids, but I thought he was going to be fine.

The nurse took our itty bittys on a "scavenger hunt" through the office so that they didn't see their Daddy being placed on a stretcher by the EMTs. *I am truly thankful for her forethought and help with that!* The kids went on their walk with the nurse, and then I spoke with the EMTs.

While I wanted to go with them in the ambulance, they wouldn't let me. That was probably a good thing, as I still had to bring our itty bittys back home and get Paulie off of the bus. I told Paul that I would meet him at the hospital as soon as I could find someone to watch our kids.

As soon as the EMTs had Paul in the ambulance, I found Noah and Sarah with the nurse and we headed home.

In the car, Noah asked, *"Why are we leaving Daddy with the doctor?"* I said, *"We need to pick Paulie up from the bus and the doctor still needs time with Daddy. I'll go back to see Daddy soon, but for now, Daddy is in good hands."*

With that question handled for the moment and both Noah and Sarah being pretty quiet, I called my dad. I asked him if he would be able to drop everything and come down to our house, which was about two hours away. I knew we would need some additional help with the kids until we had more details about what was going on. He agreed and said he would be on his way shortly.

We made it home about five minutes before Paulie's bus. I started calling and texting several neighbors and babysitters for the kids so I could get to the hospital as soon as possible. Shortly after Paulie got home, one of our neighbors was able to come over to our house so I could leave for the hospital.

Before heading to the hospital, here were the texts between Paul & I:

Paul:
Bring charger please (phone)

Me:
Will do. How are you

Threw up something fierce in ambulance

I'll be there soon. Love you.

What meds was I on

Valtrex, Medrol, Hydrocodone, Aleve

Wont give me water

Don't want u to throw up again

66/40

Blood pressure???
Trying to get sitter.
Dad is on his way.
I promise I will be there soon.
I love you.

Yep bp

Oh my!

Icu – asked if I want to be
intubated if lungs fail

> Yes. Walking in now.
> Checking you in. Be there soon.
> Love you.

Room 39

> As soon as they let me in
> I am here. I love you!

When I arrived at the Emergency Room, they wouldn't let me see Paul right away. I had to check him in and fill out the insurance paperwork. Then, I had to wait because they needed to keep a sterile environment when putting in the central line. I am not sure why it didn't hit me then just how bad this was, but I must admit that it didn't. I still thought it was a bad infection that required IV antibiotics.

While on the way to the hospital and waiting to see Paul in the ER, I spoke with most of our family and told them not to come down. We needed to get a better understanding of what we were dealing with before asking anyone for help. Paul's parents immediately headed down anyway. While I didn't want them to make this last minute trip, I was thankful they were on their way. Plus, if it were my son, I know I would do the same thing.

When I was able to see Paul, we learned his diagnosis was toxic shock syndrome (TSS) – not shingles. The Infectious Disease physician saw him in the ER and seemed very concerned. He also confirmed that we would be heading up to the ICU and he would be following Paul there. He was concerned about the infection and the lab results showing possible kidney damage. Remember those hiccups? We learned that those were signs of potential kidney failure.

An Everyday MIRACLE

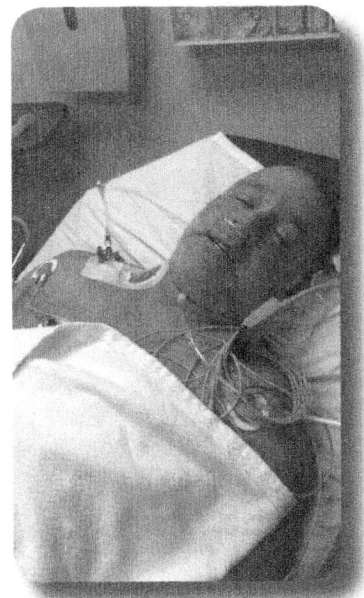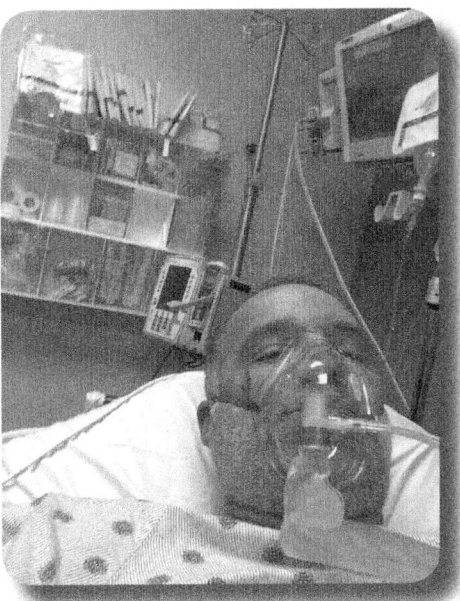

These are a couple of pictures of Paul in the ER prior to heading up to the ICU.

Thursday, February 19th, 6:30pm:

PRAYER REQUEST: Paul was rushed to the hospital this afternoon and has been diagnosed with toxic shock syndrome. He is in the ICU and is on heavy doses of antibiotics. They are worried about possible kidney damage. They assume he will be here for a few days.

Please pray for Paul. Please pray for healing and pray for healthy kidneys. Please pray for peace for Paul.

I will try to keep everyone updated, as I know more.

The heavy doses of antibiotics were all three of the biggest ones you can get – Vancomycin, Clindamycin and Zosyn. Again, having been in pharmaceuticals for over 16 years, I should have known these medications meant bad news. But, Paul was still up and talking. He was cracking jokes with the nurses and staff. I could see that he was scared, so I tried to calm him. He was in the hospital – the place where people go to get better. These doctors knew what they were doing.

Chapter 3: Needing to Breathe

Thursday, February 19, 2015: ~7:00pm

Just before 7:00pm, we arrived in the ICU. Again, Paul was cracking jokes with the nurses when a doctor came in and said he wanted to put Paul on a ventilator. While it didn't seem urgent right now, he was very concerned because of what happened during Paul's ambulance ride and time in the ER. He believed the ventilator was necessary. Paul definitely didn't want to be ventilated.

I reminded Paul of the experiences with our itty bittys. Both of our younger children were born early and needed the extra help of the NICU. Our son was placed on a ventilator first and surfactant was added to his lungs. He was able to show improvement each day.

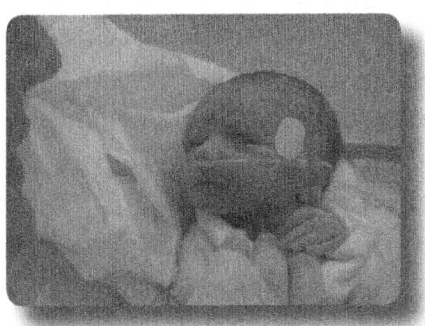

Here is our little Noah on July 21, 2010 – four days after he was born. We were so thankful he was off of the vent and we could finally hold him! Look at those tiny hands!

Our daughter was born in a different hospital, with a different doctor and a different protocol. She was started on a nasal cannula, then needed increased oxygen support, then moved to a CPAP, then again needed increased oxygen support. She never needed the ventilator, but we saw her struggle each day before she stabilized and then improved.

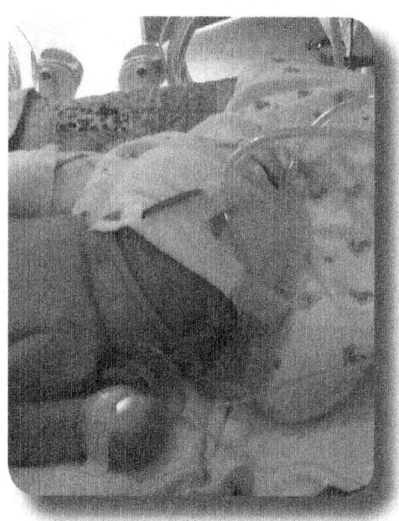

Here is our little Sarah on December 14, 2011 – two days after she was born. She was on low-stimulation because every time she woke up, she would cry and her oxygen level would drop.

While both of them are fine now and both approaches worked, I much preferred the approach with Noah. So, I told Paul I would rather him be on the ventilator and not need it (be pulled off quickly) than need it urgently and have to have a rushed procedure to get it placed. Thankfully, he agreed.

Unfortunately, it was now 7:00pm. The ICU rules were that all family members needed to be out of the unit from 7:00 - 8:30 am/pm for shift change. I told Paul I needed to go. I was going to pick up his parents and would be back by the time shift change was over, and we would be in his room at 8:30pm. I could see he was nervous, so I told him that I would be right back. That was when he said, *"Jenn, I'm scared."* I told him, *"I know you are. You are exactly where you need to be. Please don't worry. I'll be right back with your Mom & Dad."* He replied,

"I won't be here when you get back. I'll be waiting for you in Heaven."

I urgently felt the need to calm him. This wasn't that serious. He was going to be fine. At least that was what I thought. So, I quickly said, *"Paul, don't talk that way. You are going to be fine. I am going to get your parents and I will be right back."*

With that, it seemed like everything was a hustle of activity. People were coming in and out of Paul's room and they were all talking over each other. The doctors were telling me that I needed to leave. I asked the resident to step out of the room with me and asked him, *"Would you please stop talking over Paul? Please just talk to him. Paul is really scared and he doesn't understand what is being said. All of this talk is making him even more nervous."*

The resident looked at me and said, *"Your husband is really sick. We are making decisions in the room to help him. We will do the best we can."*

Again, looking back now, I guess I should have thought this was more serious than what it was, but I just thought...*this is going to be a rough few days, but he will be fine* – as stated in my first post. *A rough few days...*

I left the hospital and headed home. I called my sister, Tammy, along the way and talked with her. I was trying to make the decision on whether she and her family should come to our house to help us out for the weekend. I still didn't know what to believe. I looked up TSS on the Internet and saw that there was a 50% survival rate – that didn't sound good. But, Paul was young, otherwise healthy, and a fighter. He, of course, was on the topside of that 50%, *right?* Yet, the facts and numbers kept coming to me in the car:

> *His blood pressure was 66/40.*
> *He was in kidney failure.*
> *He was in need of a ventilator to breathe*
> **...to breathe...**

Chapter 4: This Can't be the End!

Thursday, February 19, 2015: ~7:40pm

On the drive home, I was listening to Christian radio and praying harder than I had ever prayed before.

"God, please keep my eyes on You. No assumptions here. No jumping to conclusions. Just Your Will, Your Plan. Please God, heal Paul. Take all of this away. Please!"

As you can imagine, when I arrived home, I had been crying. While I couldn't hide that, I knew I needed to be strong for our kids. Imagine what they had just gone through:

- Paulie went to school knowing his Daddy was sick. When he came home, our neighbor came over and his Mommy left for the hospital.
- Noah and Sarah were with me at the doctor's office and knew that we left Daddy there. I was supposed to be going back for him.
- Shortly after school let out, not only did Mommy leave to see Daddy in the hospital, now Grandpa was here. Busia & Papa (Paul's Mom & Dad) were here and Mommy was going to take them to see Daddy. Plus, their cousin came down from college, too.

It brings tears to my eyes to think about their little minds during that time. While I know they were happy to see everyone, they didn't know why everyone was there. *And, where was Daddy? Why wasn't he home with all of us? And, why were Mommy's eyes so red?*

I knew I needed to keep it together for the kids. So, I walked in and put the best smile on my face that I could. Paulie asked why my eyes were so red, which prompted Noah to ask the very same question. My response was the best I could come up with – *"I was listening to a sad song on the radio that made Mommy cry."* This wasn't a stretch as they had often seen me tear up in the car while listening to a good song or when watching a cartoon (yes, even cartoons can make me get a little misty). Hearing that, the boys ran into the bathroom and pulled out as much tissue as they could pull from the box, possibly the entire box. They ran to me with huge smiles, gave me the tissue – *just in case I heard more sad songs on the radio…*That made me smile and tear up at the same time.

I also needed to think about what Paulie would do the next day. It was a Friday and he was supposed to go to school. Not knowing what to expect, I told him he would have the day off of school. With everything that was running through my mind, I couldn't think about who would be there to get him on and off the bus. Plus, I wanted his day to be filled with family. I just knew Paul wouldn't be coming home within a day or two. So, I told Paulie he would have the day off to spend with family. Even though he loves school, he was pretty excited to have the day with family.

I needed to get back to the hospital. We gave everyone hugs and I took Paul's parents back to the hospital with me. I wanted to make sure we got there at 8:30pm, right when were able to get back into his room.

On the car ride to the hospital, I gave Paul's parents as much of the details as I could. I also tried to prepare them for what they were about to see. Paul would be on the ventilator when we got there. I assumed that meant Paul would be sedated, but didn't know what else to expect. Please remember, when I left the hospital, my husband was talking.

Thursday, February 19, 2015: ~8:30pm

I was not expecting what we saw when we walked back into the room.

- Paul was sedated and ventilated
- His body was twitching – almost uncontrollably

- There was an IV pole with 8 bags of medicine and fluid being pumped into him
- His fingers & toes were nearly blue
- His body was filling with fluid – by then they had already added about 8 liters of fluid (~17llbs)
- There was a nurse in his room constantly caring for him, adjusting his meds, etc.
- Plus, there were the monitors that showed:
  - Blood Pressure & Mean Arterial Pressure (MAP)
  - Respiration Rate in number, wave & stars
  - Oxygen Saturation Rate
  - Plus, the vent monitor showed the oxygen support Paul was getting

Doctors, residents, nurses and staff flowed in and out of the room, but we didn't talk much to them. When we asked questions like – *"Is this normal?"* – they didn't say much.

Paul's parents and I sat there for an hour or so talking about what was going on. We all still believed that Paul was going to be okay. He was only sedated because he didn't want to be awake with the ventilator. The antibiotics were going to work. And, he would be home very soon with all of this behind him. We believed this so very much that before 11:00pm, I told Paul's parents to go back to our house. In my mind, there was no reason for all of us to be at the hospital not getting any sleep. I would stay at the hospital with Paul and they could go back to our house to get some good sleep. I would call them if anything changed.

Soon after they left, here was my post:

Thursday, February 19th, 10:48pm:
He is vented & sedated. His kidneys aren't working and his body is in shock. Please keep praying! We need it!

Friday, February 20, 2015

Alone with Paul in his room (and the nurse in the back of the room), I watched the monitors, listened to the doctors and nurses talk to each other. I held Paul's hand. At about 12:00am, I noticed Paul's hands were really swelling up. I asked the nurse if I could remove his ring which she agreed was a good idea. I took his ring off (with some extra tugging as it was really tight) and placed it around my cross necklace where it would stay.

This is my cross with Paul's ring around it.

They had gotten Paul's sedation and pain medicines set to where he wasn't twitching as much. It seemed like he was moving in a positive direction. I didn't know much of what the monitors meant, but they didn't seem to be alarming. What I didn't know was that the nurse turned the alarms off because she was constantly monitoring his care in the room – had the alarms been on, they would have been constantly sounding.

Just before 1:00am, the doctors came into the room and said they needed to put in an arterial line into Paul's arm because they weren't getting an accurate blood pressure (plus other reasons I can no longer remember). While I wasn't completely sure what they needed to do, I remember Noah needing an arterial line when he was in the NICU. The NICU staff would continually warn us about that line, as we needed to be extra cautious about that specific line. If it was pulled out, they worried about significant bleeding. But, if Noah could handle it, Paul could handle it, too.

The doctors told me the procedure would take about forty-five minutes. They would get me in the waiting room when it was complete. So, off I went into the ICU waiting room, by myself. I made a few phone calls and learned that everyone in our entire family was on the way to the hospital or our house. My Mom and one of my sisters were already on their way. My other sister was on the way with the rest of her family (her son was the one from college already at the house with the kids). Both of Paul's sisters were on their way down. His one sister came down with her husband and two children. The other one came down with her husband, making the difficult decision to leave their two-month-old son with his other set of grandparents. Plus, one of Paul's best friends was on his way down, too. His best friend's wife called me to get the details of where we were because there was no stopping her husband.

As I sat there in the ICU waiting room, I was grateful others were coming. I felt very alone and scared. That said, I didn't know if we needed all of them there. We didn't know what we were dealing with or how long it would take for Paul to get better. We didn't know when we would be bringing him home or what he would need when he got home. While I was grateful, I was hoping we weren't getting all of the support now when we might need much more of it at a later time.

As I look back now, I didn't sit much; instead, I paced. I paced back and forth in the waiting room. I kept looking down the hall to see if the doctors were coming. I walked to the unit doors to peek down the hall to see if the curtain in his room was open – the sign that I could go back into the room. Especially after the forty-five minutes had past, I wanted to be with Paul, and I was pacing.

It was also during this time that I sent an e-mail to my team leader, letting him know that I would be out "indefinitely." I gave a brief summary of what was going on with Paul, and how his situation had changed. I told him I would be in touch sometime in the next week to discuss what was needed on the projects I was working on, but not to expect much from me the next few weeks – or at least until we had a better handle on what was going on. It's funny how just one-week prior, I was so nervous about what was to happen with my job, and the very next week, my job was the least of my worries. I just needed to focus on Paul. And, I needed to get back into his room. *Why was this taking so long?*

It was just before 2:00am when the resident came to get me. We were walking toward Paul's room, and I was asking him about the procedure, how it went, etc. As he was sharing the information with me, I remember stopping in the hall, looking him in the eye and asking him, *"What is going on with my husband? I know everyone keeps saying he is sick, and I see that. But, what is going on? What should I expect? What are we looking at here? I mean, it's not like he is circling the drain or something."*

While I will again always be sorry for that last statement, I think it shows where my mind was at that time. I knew he was sick, but hospitals were places people went to get better. I mean, seriously, my husband was a healthy and strong man. He was playing basketball last weekend. He was just making jokes with the nurses seven hours ago. I knew this was serious, but what were we looking at? What were we to expect?

I will never forget these words for as long as I live. The resident stopped, put his hand on my shoulder and said,

"We have a lot of sick patients in the hospital. Right now, your husband is the sickest patient we have. And, I do not know if he will make it through the night. I think it would be best if you would call your family. He may not have much time left."

I felt the world stop in that very moment. It was like I was watching everything around me, but I wasn't there. As I write this now, I can't stop the tears. It's hard to breathe. I feel this lump in my throat and a pain in my chest. It was real. It hit me. My husband could die. Not just could die, the doctors believed that he would die.

On my way back into the room, I called Paul's parents. I don't remember what I said to them. I remember saying something about it being time to come back to the hospital. They asked me a question, but I couldn't respond. I just said come up and come now. We hung up. It would be ~30 minutes before they could get there. I was praying Paul would last that long.

All alone in his room, these words were filling my head:

"He may not have much time left!"

What? This isn't happening. What does that mean? This cannot be real. Where is everyone? Why am I alone? Please, God! Don't let this be true...

While I was waiting for Paul's parents to arrive, I added this post:

> **Friday, February 20th, 2:10am:**
> Please pray now. He is crashing!

My Dad, seeing this, sent a text that he was on his way to the hospital. Our nephew would stay at the house with the kids and let them sleep. Plus, the kids weren't allowed in the hospital anyway due to a flu restriction. The rest of the family were on their way to the house or hospital.

I sat there in his room, alone, crying, not knowing what to do next. A respiratory therapist came into the room, sat next to me, rubbed my back while I broke down. She wanted to make sure I wasn't alone during that time. I am still so very thankful for that. She didn't need to do that. She had other work to do. But, instead, she sat with me so I wasn't alone.

It was about this time I asked for someone to come up and pray with us. The hospital chaplain was soon in Paul's room with a Bible, rosary, and lots of love and prayers. We prayed together as we waited for our parents to arrive. They also called for a priest and he would soon be on his way up. He was asked to *"please hurry..."*

The nurse looked at me and asked, *"How long will it take for your family to get here?"* She didn't know they were already called. I said they were at our house about thirty minutes away and were already on their way back to the hospital. She nodded and went back to watching monitors to do her part to keep Paul alive until the family arrived.

After some time, Paul's parents arrived. The chaplain was still in there praying with me for Paul. His parents had a lot of questions. I answered them the best I could, but unfortunately, I didn't have many answers. Paul's dad was instantly on his knees next to Paul's bed praying. Paul's mom and I were sitting next to Paul's bed, holding his hands in disbelief. Well, it was shock really. We were fully in shock. We just kept saying – *this can't be. This can't be.*

When the priest arrived, he asked if he should pray and if we wanted Paul to be anointed. Around that time, my dad and Paul's best friend had also made it into the room. We were all there, standing around the bed, praying with the priest while Paul was given Last Rites (also called anointing of the sick – it is a sacrament of the Catholic Church given to a person who is gravely sick).

I am not sure who arrived next and in what order. I just know that soon we had a room full of people. In a room where there are only to be two visitors at a time, there were at least 4-6 people in there at all times that night. I guess the rules are more flexible when they don't believe the patient will live more than a few hours.

With everyone there, I asked for the doctors to come in. I still didn't truly understand what we were waiting for and I was looking for answers. When the doctors arrived, here was what we learned:

- Paul had toxic shock syndrome (TSS)
- While the survival rate of TSS is 50%, Paul was at the bottom of that percentage...very bottom
- He was in multi-organ failure, and they were doing all they could do medically to help him
- The next twenty-four hours were critical as he would need to survive at least that long for the antibiotics to work

They had done, medically, all that they could do. It was up to Paul now.

Their main concern was keeping Paul's blood pressure up. It was still in the 60-something / 40-50 something. His mean arterial pressure (or MAP) was still in the low 50s. At the time, we were told the goal was to get this above 60 and keep it stable from there. We would later learn the goal is actually above 65, but they were giving us a smaller goal as they didn't believe he would even make it to 60. The two ways they have to keep a patient's blood pressure up are:

- Pushing IV fluids and/or
- Using medicines called pressors

With Paul, they were already pushing a lot of fluid through his IV, but the fluid was moving out of his vessels and into the rest of his body. This was becoming quite obvious as his body was blowing up with fluid. It looked like a pin would pop him and fluid would come out of everywhere. We were told this was normal, but he definitely didn't look normal.

As for the pressors, Paul was already maxed out on four pressors and his MAP was still only in the low 50s. They weren't sure how long these medicines would give him before his heart would give out. So, medically, they had done everything.

What does that mean? I remember asking the question. Well, I guess it was more of a statement. I said to the doctors, *"I don't get it. You are telling me my husband is just going to die."*

To that, the resident (the same one who told me to call the family) said, *"Well, I guess he has a chance."*

What? He has a <u>chance</u>? Please tell me this isn't happening!

The one additional option was for the Infectious Disease doctor to add IV Immunoglobulin (IVIG). It was a medicine that would help Paul's immune system and was considered a "last ditch effort." So, I asked that the medicine be rushed up for Paul and then let the doctors go. I just didn't want to hear any more of their numbers or statistics, and they didn't have anything left to say to us. As they said, they had done everything medically that they could do. It was now up to Paul.

As they left, Paul's mom grabbed my hand. We were sitting at Paul's side and we were both sobbing. She said, *"This can't be. This isn't the end. He can't die. He has too much to live for. You have three kids at home that need their Dad. What will we do? He can't die. It's not time. He has too much to live for."*

My response to Paul's mom was, *"This isn't the way this will end. God's not done with Paul, and neither are we. He has too much to fight for. He is not giving up, so we are not giving up. God's got this. Paul's got this. We are going to stay positive and pray!"*

At that moment, I knew that the doctors were wrong. Well, at least they were partly wrong. This wasn't just up to Paul; this was really up to God. He had the power to take all of this away, to pull my husband away from the brink of death and provide complete healing. The God that I had come to know, the God of my understanding, was a miracle-worker. He was a God that moves mountains; He was a God who parts seas. He was an ever-living God that could heal Paul. And, that was what we needed to focus on – praying for God to heal Paul!

Chapter 5: Everyone Near and Far, "Please Pray!"

Friday, February 20, 2015: ~5:00am

Since we couldn't see what was going on inside of Paul's body, we watched the monitors, specifically the MAP. That was the measure we could focus on to see if the medicines, and the prayers, were working. We were praying for that number to move up and remain steady. And, we knew we couldn't do it alone. We had started this journey asking for prayer support, and we needed continual prayer support. Here was what I posted:

> **Friday, February 20th, 5:38am:**
> Paul is in multi-organ failure.
>
> Trying to keep him stable for the antibiotics to work so that his systems can turn back on. Please continue to pray!!

And, that was what we did until we needed to leave the room for shift change. We prayed. We kept each other focused on the positive, or at least not spiraling on the negative – as it was so easy to focus on the negative. When one of us in the room would break, someone was there to pick that person up. We prayed, we watched the monitors, and then we prayed some more.

Here is where it gets a little foggy on timing. The nephrologist (kidney doctor) had been around to see us, but I am not exactly sure when. We knew that Paul was in acute kidney failure and he would eventually need dialysis to: (1) filter out the toxins and (2) remove the excess fluid from his body. The problem was, with the pressors topped out at maximum dosage, if the dialysis caused Paul's blood pressure to drop at all, there weren't many options to help him and his heart could give out.

The nephrologist explained that while she knew he would need a dialysis port placed, she also wanted him more stable so he could better handle that procedure. She wanted to prepare me for what needed to happen and why it was necessary.

During the 7:00 – 8:30am shift change, the nephrologist came out to the waiting room to talk with us. She reminded us of the importance of dialysis, and confirmed Paul still wasn't stable enough to actually start the dialysis. That said, she did believe there would soon be a window to surgically place the dialysis port. That way, when Paul was stable enough, they could start the dialysis. She walked us through the procedure – the radiologist would do this in Paul's room. It would be a relatively short procedure to place the port, and then they would do an x-ray to ensure the port was in the right place and ready for the dialysis to start whenever Paul's body was ready. As I did with the ventilator, I agreed that it was better to place it as soon as possible, so they could start the dialysis as soon as he was stable enough.

I also appreciated the support from a friend of my sister's family who was also a nephrologist. I was able to talk with him about Paul's status and discuss the steps the doctors were taking. What I truly appreciated about our conversations was that he never second guessed Paul's doctors. He listened, gave me things to watch for, encouraged me to keep positive, and committed that he and his wife would continue praying. I will forever be thankful for that.

Friday, February 20, 2015: ~8:30am
We were waiting at the ICU door for the clock to turn to 8:30am. We ran into Paul's room to see so many IVs and medicine lines. He had needed an additional pole of medicines to be hooked up, so when we returned, he had two full IV poles with eight lines each. That's sixteen lines of medicine and fluids! Not to mention the ventilator, and the orogastric (OG) tube going down his throat that was pulling the acid from his stomach. Plus, he was given a catheter when he arrived in the

ICU. Unfortunately, he hadn't produced much, if any urine. Just imagine – all that fluid and little to no urine output. My husband was blowing up. And, there was nothing they could do to relieve it because he needed all of the support.

For the next two hours, we sat there and prayed. And, we watched the MAP. We started to see small improvements in the numbers. It went up to 54 and stayed steady. Then, it was up to 55. About an hour later, we saw a 56. The rapid decline had stopped and he seemed to be stabilizing. Paul was still <u>the sickest person in the hospital</u>, but he was no longer in rapid decline.

Considering the need for dialysis and his apparent stabilization, the nephrologist came back and recommended it was time to have the dialysis port surgically placed. If I agreed, she would call radiology and get it ordered. Based on our conversations, I agreed and she went to place the order.

As she left the ICU waiting room, a family member asked several questions that were likely on the minds of other family members. The questions were, *"Are we just delaying the inevitable? Should we continue with this? What are the chances Paul will make it through this? Are we doing more harm than good?"*

While I fully believed we should move forward with the procedure, I agreed these were good questions to ask. Truly, we didn't want to do extra, unnecessary harm. We just wanted to save him. But, looking at him in that bed, the odds of him surviving did not look good. And, up to this point, no doctor had given us any hope of a positive outcome.

So, a few of us walked back over to the nephrologist and asked the questions, *"Do you believe this is worth it? Are we causing him unneeded pain or harm? Do you think this will work?"*

Her answer was so helpful. She had a family member with toxic shock syndrome who made it through (God moment!). And, her words were the most positive and encouraging we had heard thus far. She said, in reference to Paul, *"He is young and was healthy before this. He has both of those things going for him. He definitely has a chance to get through this. You should do everything you can to save him."*

She was the first medical professional to tell us he had a chance. I'm not sure she realized it at that time, but that was exactly what was needed. Someone who had some experience with a person surviving this infection, and someone in the medical profession to give the entire family some additional hope. Truly, this was such a God moment! We may not have realized it at the time, but she was the perfect physician to be working that weekend.

Here was my next post:

> **Friday, February 20th, 10:49am:**
> Thank you everyone! Please keep praying.
>
> Paul is running 104.4 fever and they know they need to start dialysis sometime soon.
>
> Radiology coming up to place port.
>
> Keeping him sedated.
>
> He looks more comfortable than before.

Yes. You read that correctly. His temperature was 104.4 degrees. As I am writing this, it is hard to believe that we were not even twenty-four hours into this journey. At that time, it felt like it had been days already. And, we had no idea when this would end – or what the outcome would be. So, I kept my focus on the present, the positive, and the prayers.

What was amazing about Facebook and other social media outlets was how quickly we were able to mobilize a community of people to pray for Paul. What I haven't added to the posts were all the likes and comments from family and friends, plus personal messages, texts, phone calls, flowers, cards, etc. We had more prayer warriors praying for Paul than any of us could ever imagine – already, within 24 hours! So, those who were far away were able to stay just as connected as those who were close-by.

Another one of Paul's very good friends from high school lived pretty close to us. He was reading the posts about Paul basically from the beginning. He was sending messages because he works in the medical field and knew many of the doctors in the area. He was planning to come to the hospital that morning to see us. He had been on the phone all night and morning with his medical colleagues and confirmed we were in the best place. Just as I was reading the message from him that he was on his way, I looked up and there he was in the ICU waiting room. What was also amazing was that he actually knew the doctor placing Paul's port. So, as we walked into Paul's room, Paul's friend introduced me to the doctor who did the procedure. He confirmed the procedure went well, and Paul would be ready for dialysis whenever he was stable enough to get started.

When I turned the corner to enter Paul's room, another doctor stopped me in the hall. While he wasn't on Paul's case, he had heard about Paul's story from a Bible study group he was in with a great friend of mine. He was stopping by to see if there was anything he could do for us and to let us know he was praying...along with many others.

What was amazing was how quickly people responded and wanted to help. Remember when I mentioned how blessed we were to have great neighbors? Within hours of hearing about Paul's hospitalization, another great friend & neighbor, had already stared a meal train. And, within hours of starting it, it was nearly full through the end of April. Our neighbors, family, friends & some people who barely knew our family committed to bringing us meals every other day from mid-February to the end of April. I truly mean within hours, it was full! What a blessing to know that meals for the family were taken care of! Especially because we had no idea when this trial would end or what the outcome would be.

I also needed to process that I wasn't going to be home for some time. While I didn't know how long, I just knew it would be a while. Everyone was willing to stay at the hospital or at the house until we had more information. Paul's parents said they would stay, as would Paul's sisters. While it was great to have them stay, I knew they would all want to be at the hospital – it was their son, their brother lying in that bed. My parents would stay for a few days; meaning my one sister would need to go back to take care of their business. The rest of the family, our brother-in-laws and nieces & nephews would need to get back home Sunday or Monday for work and school.

While I completely understood, I was worried about our little ones. I needed someone to be able to focus on our kids so that I could focus on Paul at the hospital. I knew our friends and neighbors would all want to help; however, I couldn't even figure out what we needed at home or how to put together a schedule to make that work. It was too much for me to even think about organizing. Without a second thought, my sister Tammy started to move her obligations so that she would be able to be at the house with our kids. She would provide a stable home for our three children for as long as she was needed. And, she would help identify opportunities for our friends and neighbors to help. I was then, am now, and will forever be so very grateful for that! That allowed me to spend my time focused on Paul and his needs.

I was there for every doctor visit to Paul's room, and I asked the nurse a lot of questions. She was the first to tell me, if she wasn't nervous, I shouldn't be nervous. The doctors and nurses walked me through what we might expect next. It was about this time that I realized what they had been saying...there wasn't a typical 40-year-old male with toxic shock syndrome. While I was scared and looking for answers, the hospital staff were also not used to seeing someone like Paul. They were also hoping for a positive outcome for him and trying everything they knew to do in order to keep him alive. I think this helped me to keep a very positive perspective as they were looking at data that didn't pertain to Paul because Paul was an anomaly. He didn't fit their data. So, instead of focusing on statistics, I remained focused on Paul, on the MAP, and on praying for him to heal.

It was again time for us to leave Paul's room for shift change. Here was my update:

> **Friday, February 20th, 7:10pm:**
> UPDATE: He has gotten better throughout the day. His temp is down and his blood pressure is better (with lots of medicine help).
>
> His kidneys are still not working - may start dialysis tomorrow. Port is already placed for that.
>
> They are also worried about his lungs as the next organ to fail.
>
> Please keep praying. While he has improved some, he still has a long road to recovery. And, we are only focused on recovery.

While I wrote the post this way, all of the doctors were still telling us that Paul was still in very critical condition. Most still felt the likelihood of Paul surviving was not very good at all. The fact he made it through the first twenty-four hours was a good sign...truly, *a miracle*. However, it was not a sign he was "out of the woods". Here were some of the reasons they kept classifying Paul as being in **very critical condition:**

Lungs:
They were ordering a chest x-ray because, while the oxygen level on the monitor looked low but acceptable, Paul's blood gas test showed the transfer of oxygen from the lungs into the blood was not efficient. It was below 60% where the goal was high 90s at least. They didn't believe the oxygen was getting to his organs and were very concerned. They had been telling me

that could happen, and there was a protocol, if it did happen. However, we definitely didn't want it to happen.

Blood pressure support:
Paul was no longer requiring bolus IV fluids, which was good because he had already received about twenty liters of fluid (yes, that's 44lbs). And, since his pressure was stabilizing without the bolus IV fluid, they had started to lower the dose of one of the pressors. Thankfully, Paul's blood pressure was holding on.

Kidneys:
Paul was not making urine. I think he might have made ~50mL of urine. Considering most people make over 1500mL of urine in a day, 50mL since being admitted was not good. And, the urine he was producing was definitely not normal. It was dark and cloudy. Plus, with all of the fluid they were adding to him to keep his blood pressure up, his lack of urine production made dialysis more urgent.

Liver:
As to be expected, Paul's liver function results were showing significant impairment. The challenge with that was that many of Paul's medicines needed to be metabolized (broken down) by the liver. With his liver function impaired, this was a potential challenge to keep his medicines appropriately dosed. Plus, since many medicines are cleared from the body through the kidneys and urination, there were excess medicines sticking around longer in his body, as he wasn't able to clear them through the "normal" way we usually clear medicine. While the pharmacists know all of this and deal with it all the time, it was still a concern.

Considering all of this, the nephrologist came back in to see us. She believed it was time to start the dialysis. She felt better about starting it now because, if Paul needed extra blood pressure support, they could increase the dose of the pressor they just pulled off. This gave her some flexibility and comfort, and we agreed it was time to start. Here was my next post:

> **Friday, February 20th, 9:40pm:**
> UPDATE: Paul's lungs have started to become impaired. Looks like the starting of Adult Respiratory Distress Syndrome. This was somewhat expected.
>
> They also believe it is time to start dialysis. They will start that tonight.
>
> Please pray that he handles the transition to the dialysis.
> Please pray that his pressure stabilizes and they can pull off some of this fluid.
> Please pray that the lung damage that we see is as minimal as possible.
> And please pray for his liver. They are seeing signs of failure, which can challenge their ability to keep Paul sedated and calm.
> Please pray he can stay sedated and calm.

After I wrote this, I started talking to Paul. I thought about how important it would be to talk to him instead of talking around him. When he was awake, I knew how others talking over him would really bother him. Now that he was "sleeping", I didn't know what he could hear and understand. So, if he could understand anything, I wanted him to hear it from me.

Here was what I said to him,

"Paul, I love you! I want you to know that I have all of the medical decisions covered. I am asking all of the questions and learning as much as I can to make the best decisions for you. Right now, you need to rest. You need to let the medicines work and let your body heal.

*You **are not** allowed to go anywhere but here! If you see a light, you tell God you are not ready, I am not ready, and I am not letting you go! You tell Him to change His plan and let you stay here with me.*

You have so much more to do here with us. And, we need you. Right now, we need you to rest. Let the medicine work and let your body heal."

Then, it hit me. God had always had a plan, and that plan may not have included Paul coming home with me. Right then and there that I started praying for God's plan to be, specifically, that Paul and I would be walking out of the hospital together. We would be walking out of this hospital, hand-in-hand, going home together to our kids. I needed that prayer because, regardless of what God's plan originally was, I needed it to be that Paul was going to be completely healed and coming home with me. I wanted to be as specific as possible to ensure there was no miscommunication.

I needed Paul COMPLETELY HEALED!

Chapter 6: Holding Our Breath

Friday, February 20, 2015: ~10:00pm
Paul's dad asked if I had called the church yet to let them know about Paul's condition. I was grateful he reminded me to make that call, as I knew the church would lift up additional prayers for Paul. So, during one of my few trips out of Paul's room, I left a message for the church. I asked that they add Paul to the prayer list, and I would keep them updated as we learned more about Paul's condition. I was thankful to have another great avenue for additional prayer support for Paul. He definitely needed them!

Just after 10:30pm, the dialysis technician arrived to start Paul's dialysis. Since I didn't know what to expect, I was nervous that this could be difficult for him to handle. I was worried about his blood pressure. I was worried about his sedation & pain. Let's just say, I was worried about *everything*. Here were my next two posts:

> **Friday, February 20th, 10:47pm:**
> Starting dialysis

> **Friday, February 20th, 11:02pm:**
> Transition to dialysis went well. He will be on a slow, continuous dialysis
>
> Oxygen levels are low - too low. So, they did all they can with the vent and will be starting protocol for Adult Respiratory Distress Syndrome. Will send note when I learn more.

What a difficult fifteen minutes! We were so thankful that the transition to dialysis went smoothly. I don't think there was even a small change in the monitor numbers for his blood pressure, heart rate, etc. He handled that transition very well. Praise God!

That said, the doctors were now very concerned about his oxygen levels. They told me about Adult Respiratory Distress Syndrome (ARDS). From what I understood, that was when the lungs would become stiff and have difficultly expanding and contracting. If that happened, it would be very challenging for Paul to breathe and would require an entirely new protocol.

While we were waiting for the results of the chest x-ray, here was my next post:

> **Friday, February 20th, 11:13pm:**
> Please keep praying. They are working

Looking back now, I wish I had been more specific with the writing of my prayer request. I was specifically praying for the chest x-ray to show that Paul's lungs were not showing signs of ARDS. I was praying that the reason for the lack of oxygenation in his blood was due to some other reason than ARDS and the x-ray would prove that.

Within thirty minutes, we got the results of the chest x-ray. As you know, God didn't need the specific prayers; He knew exactly what we were praying for. Here was the post after we received the results of the chest x-ray:

> **Friday, February 20th, 11:45pm:**
> Chest x-ray was better than expected. Still not great but better than they thought.
> Still not getting great oxygen. Upped vent and waiting 1 hour.

This was the first time there was an expected setback that Paul didn't have. Everyone expected that we would be starting the ARDS protocol, but that was not needed. Please know, they were fully prepared to start the protocol. And, just because *this* x-ray did not show the need to start the protocol immediately, the doctors still believed it was quite likely we would be experiencing this setback sometime soon. But, for now, we didn't need to worry about that.

That was the best news we could have gotten. And, we were all completely wiped. We had been up for nearly forty-eight hours and had barely eaten a thing. We definitely needed our rest, but no one wanted to sleep. We didn't want to miss a minute of being with Paul because that minute could be our last. However, we all knew we were not going to be able to stay up much longer.

We agreed to take shifts that night. We would each try to sleep some while others would spend time with Paul. Plus, we had such a great nurse that agreed to let us know if anything changed with him. She was very worried about all of us and wanted to ensure we got our sleep. If Paul made it through this, he would need us to be strong. We needed to focus on ourselves, too. So, I agreed to sleep for a few hours. I would be back in Paul's room by 6:00am to spend time with Paul and talk with the nurse before shift change.

As I walked out into the ICU waiting room, I realized this would be my home for a while…at least I hoped it would be a while, as that would mean Paul would still be alive. We had already started to set up camp in an area where we had a few blankets and sheets. We were so very thankful the hospital had allowed us to borrow some for the night. We would need to have someone bring more from the house. We were also very thankful that a neighbor, the same one who watched the kids when I left for the ER, dropped off two camping mattresses earlier in the day. That gave us more options for everyone to sleep during their "off" shifts.

Saturday, February 21, 2015

During the night, the nurse was drawing a blood gas, which was a test to measure the acidity, oxygen and carbon dioxide in Paul's blood. She was assuming it wasn't going to be good – meaning Paul's lungs were more impaired and the ARDS protocol would likely be needed. Based on all of the previous information, there was no reason to believe it was going to be good. When she received the lab results, Paul's sisters were in the room, and the nurse seemed nervous to look at them.

However, when she saw the numbers, she was surprised – in a good way. She had a huge smile on her face when she shared the news with Paul's sisters. The numbers were much better than expected and she was truly pleased about the progress Paul was making. His sisters came out and shared that news with those who were awake in the waiting room. They let me sleep for a couple more hours, knowing that the news could wait – and I needed some sleep.

Chapter 7: What Do I Say to our Kids?

Saturday, February 21, 2015: ~6:00am

When I woke up, a friend from college was in the ICU waiting room. She was an ER physician at that very hospital and was starting her morning shift. We had been texting so she knew the basic information of what was going on with Paul, but wanted to stop by to see if there was anything she could do for us. I filled her in on Paul's updated status, and I shared my concern about what to say to our children – especially our oldest son, Paulie. He would be going back to school on Monday. Some of the students would know of Paul's condition because we were Facebook friends with their parents. I wanted to protect his heart – all of their hearts and minds. She recommended I connect with another college friend of ours who went through a similar experience just few years before.

Our friend's husband was also in the ICU of that very same hospital. She had to decide what to share with their little ones – what was enough / what was too much. And, as soon as she heard about Paul, she got in touch with me to let me know she was there and they were all praying. So, while we knew she would want to help, we also knew that it would open up some deep emotions. I knew I could learn a lot from her experience, but I really didn't want to put her in the situation to need to talk about it again. That said, she was the only other person I knew that had gone through anything similar. So, I prayed about it as we walked into Paul's room.

We entered the room at about 6:00am. The nurse beamed as she shared the news about Paul's blood gas numbers; I could see the excitement in her eyes. The numbers were good! Not just okay, but they looked really good! She was the first nurse to tell me point blank, *"I wanted to do everything I could to keep your husband alive.*" All of the nurses, doctors and staff wanted to do the same thing. They definitely didn't want to lose Paul on their shift, but it was more than that. He was sick – *I mean really sick*. And, they wanted to take care of him the best they could so that he would survive...not just their shift. They cared for him, too. He was more than just a patient to them. They heard his story. They knew he was an amazing husband, father, son, brother, in-law, friend, etc. They wanted him to live. And, they were doing everything in their power to make sure he did. Not just because it was their job, it was personal.

During shift change, this was my post:

> **Saturday, February 21st, 8:14am:**
> UPDATE: He had a good night.
>
> The dialysis is working. They are able to pull the fluids they are giving him. Plus, they were able to take off 1 blood pressure med and his BP is holding strong.
>
> The first creatinine (a kidney function lab) reading after starting dialysis showed improvement - from 7.5 to 6.5. The goal is back around 1.
>
> His blood oxygen level has increased to 107 so they were able to bring his oxygen percent back down to 80% but still needing lots of help expanding his lungs. Yesterday, it had dropped to 54, so they had to up his oxygen to 100% and increase the pressure to open his lungs.
>
> Our next concern is the rash. The one on his back is starting to slough off. They will switch his bed to make it easier to watch & clean. The two worries with this are infection and the potential fluid loss. This can affect his blood pressure so having the one pressor completely off gives us room to add it if needed.

> They will wake him up a bit today to ensure he can wake up and then put him back to sleep. I have asked to be in there to see his eyes.
>
> I appreciate the prayers for all of the family. We all did sleep a bit & they kept him alive and some small improvements.
>
> I'll send more when I know. Thank you for continued prayers.

After writing that post, I knew it was time to go home. A few of us decided to go, and my brother-in-law offered to drive. I wasn't really in any shape to drive.

While I didn't want to leave Paul, I knew I needed to see the kids and talk with them. They woke up on Friday to a house full of family, and everyone was going back and forth to the hospital. They were having fun with their cousins, but they were starting to ask questions. It was time for me to go home and be with them. I was praying about what to say to them when I decided to text my friend whose husband had a similar experience to see if she would be able to talk. Of course, she made the time. So, on my way home, she and I were able to connect.

It was an emotional call for both of us. She was the only person that knew what it felt like to be there in the ICU with your husband, your best friend, fighting for his life. She knew what it felt like to be in a room full of people, and still feel very alone. She knew what it felt like to know that your children needed you and your husband needed you. She knew what it felt like to try to put on a strong face for your children when your heart was broken because you did not know and could not control the outcome. She knew.

I am so sorry that she went through what she did. I am so sorry she had to feel that pain, that emotional roller coaster, that sadness. There really are NO words to describe how that feels. I pray no one has to go through a similar journey. That said, she was grateful she could help me through my journey and we would both be there if anyone else had a similar experience.

Another blessing was that both she and I have a very strong faith in God. So, we could talk very openly about our faith during this most difficult time. I am truly thankful for that.

Just hearing her voice and knowing their outcome, we both knew it was possible that Paul could survive this. She shared so much with me that morning. Here was the piece of advice that only she could share,

"Don't make any promises you can't keep. Don't promise Daddy is coming home, and don't make any promises about God. While you can hold onto that hope and pray Paul will come home, we don't know God's plans are for Paul. So, you don't want to promise something that might not happen."

That was so very true. The last thing I wanted was to make a promise to the kids, have Paul not make it through this, and have them mad at me and God for failing to live up to my promises. I could not imagine what that would feel like, to lose my husband and then to lose our children's trust in me and in God. I would not have thought of that, and was so very grateful she shared those words with me.

We finished talking for a few minutes. She said she would be praying for us, and specifically for me. If there was anything she could do, she wanted me to know she was there – right down the street. She also offered to come up to the hospital. While I appreciated the offer, I knew that would be very emotional. I could never ask her to do that. With that, we said our good-byes and I walked into our house.

When I came into the house, the kids ran up and gave me huge hugs. They were playing with their cousins and were pretty distracted. I told them I was going to head upstairs to take a shower (I needed this time to ready myself for our conversation), and I thought it would be a great idea for them to make posters and pictures for Daddy's walls. I asked them to do this and went upstairs. While they were busy making art, I was breaking down in the shower and then packing up items I would need with me at the hospital.

As I walked downstairs, I first stopped in my office to pack up my computer – I was going to need to get some work done, or at least make it easier to post updates on Paul's progress. While in there, I saw a book I was given a few weeks prior at a women's Christian retreat called, "Soul Spa Sisterhood".

> **Background: Soul Spa Sisterhood**
>
> *My friend, the one who knew the Infectious Disease doctor, and I were trying to find a morning to grab a cup of coffee and catch up. I loved spending time with her, as she understood my life better than most. She was the primary breadwinner of her family and had a position that required a great deal of travel, too. She was also a very strong Christian, and I had learned so very much from her in my walk with Jesus. So, as we were looking for times to connect, the date of this retreat came up – January 30th. She invited me to join her, but the retreat was from morning to early afternoon. I remember wanting to go, but not thinking that I could swing it. Again, I was very concerned that my position at work would be eliminated. While my schedule was usually crazy, it seemed the beginning of the year was especially busy due to this pending announcement. So, I didn't believe I would be able to get the time off for the entire morning, but when I looked at my calendar, it was wide-open. Another amazing God moment! I blocked my calendar as "tentative" for the time and hoped nothing more "pressing" came up.*
>
> *As the morning drew closer, my calendar was still clear. I knew that God had made it possible for me to attend this retreat. So, I took the day off and was looking forward to spending time in fellowship with other amazing Christian women. While I called it a day off, I knew I had to work that afternoon, including a call with our team leader. However, I would go to the breakfast guilt-free and spend a few much-needed hours with God.*

When I made it to the breakfast, I realized that I had another connection to the host. I had met her husband two years earlier when I had started purposeful networking. Even back then, I had a feeling my job might be in jeopardy, so I started connecting with area business leaders. Her husband was both as a successful business leader and an alumnus of my alma mater. He was the one who introduced me to the friend who invited me to the retreat...it all came full-circle. Little did he know that the person he connected me with for business would do so much more for me spiritually and personally. I still need to thank him for that.

So, here I was at this amazing women's breakfast with nearly sixty other women, and the leader had ten books she was giving away. She had written up questions for the group to answer by raising their hands, and she would select the first woman's hand she saw to give away the book. I had raised my hand for the question, "Who needs to go back to work this afternoon?" As previously mentioned, I actually had to walk out of the session the minute it ended to jump on a call with my team leader. Even though it was a vacation day, there were a few things we needed to discuss which would then require additional action on my part.

I remember when she gave me the book I thought – I should give this to someone else. I travel a lot, and I don't usually bring books with me on the plane. I should give this to someone and download the book onto my iPad. But, for some reason, I decided to keep the book. Little did I know that less than three weeks later, I would be in a hospital with my husband, needing quiet time with God and wanting a physical book to read. The book she gave me was <u>Soul Keeping, Caring for the Most Important Part of You</u> by John Ortberg.

When I walked into my office to grab my computer bag and my laptop, that book was sitting on top of a stack of books and papers. It was the first thing I saw, and I couldn't take my eyes off of it. God knew I needed that book. And, He ensured I had it to read when I needed it the most. So, I added it to my bag and walked into the kitchen.

When I walked into the kitchen, Noah asked, *"How long will it be until Daddy comes home?"* I took in a deep breath and prayed for God to give me the right answers for the kids. I thought about my previous conversation – <u>no promises</u>.

So, I brought the kids into our bedroom and talked with all of them about what their Daddy was going through. Here was what I remember saying to them, *"I'm not really sure. Daddy is at the hospital, and the doctors are doing everything they can to help make Daddy better. Daddy can use extra prayers right now. So, whenever you are missing your Daddy, please pray that God heals him. Mommy will be spending lots of time with Daddy at the hospital, so Aunt Tammy will be here with you guys. Please know I am only a phone call away, okay?"*

What I love about little ones is that their minds seem to shift very quickly. Our itty bittys said, *"okay"* and went back to playing with their cousins. That was a good enough answer for them.

I asked Paulie to sit with me for a few more minutes. I asked him if he had any questions. He said he didn't. I could see in his eyes that his mind was spinning. I wanted to say something to comfort him, but I didn't want to make any promises. And, I knew he would be going to school on Monday where other kids might ask him questions. I remembered my friend talking about that experience with her boys, so I shared a similar message with Paulie. I said, *"Paulie, when you go to school on Monday, some kids might ask you about your Daddy. Mommy has let some of their parents know what is going on, so some of your friends might know. Please know this. If they are asking you about your Daddy that just means that they are praying for Daddy at their homes. They are praying for him to get better. Right now, your Daddy needs lots of prayers. We are so very thankful your friends and families are praying."*

He looked at me with his big, loving eyes and said *"okay"*. He gave me a huge hug and said he understood. I told him I needed to go back to the hospital, and he left the room to play with his cousins.

I pulled myself together, walked back into the kitchen and got ready to go back to the hospital. I was grabbing paperwork and bills when I came across a birthday party invitation for a friend of Paulie's. The birthday was the next Sunday afternoon. While I wasn't sure about much, I had a feeling Paul wouldn't be home by then. So, I pulled Paulie aside and told him, *"I don't think you are going to be able to go to this birthday party. I am just not sure how we can get it all worked out."*

His big eyes looked back up at me and he asked, *"So, you don't think Dad will be home by then?"* My heart broke as I looked right back at him and said, *"No buddy, I don't think so."*

Seeing the look on his face, I knew that I needed to work this out. We had plenty of people willing to help. So, I added, *"But, let me see what I can do to help make this all work out."*

He shook his head and went to find his cousins again. It absolutely broke my heart. He needed to have a sense of normalcy. Without a second thought, my sister took the invitation and said she would ensure we could work this out. Paulie would be able to go, and I didn't need to worry about it. She would handle all of it. *Thank you!*

I knew it was time for us to get back to the hospital. We hadn't been home for much more than an hour, yet it felt like it was too long. I needed to get back to Paul. And, I didn't have anything else to say to the kids to make it better. I couldn't bring their Daddy home, and I couldn't be strong any longer. So, we wrapped up their artwork and notes, gave lots of hugs and kisses, and then we drove back to the hospital. I think I cried every second of that 30-minute drive. I cried and I prayed.

"Please God! Please heal Paul. Please make your plan that Paul comes home with me, walking hand in hand, coming home to take care of our babies. Please God. No matter what your original plan was – please make that your plan. We need him. I need him. Please!"

Chapter 8: Keeping Our Focus on God and His Miracles

Saturday, February 21, 2015: ~1:00pm
Back at the hospital, we had family and several friends stop by to visit. I felt it was important to help them prepare for what they were about to see. Paul looked very different than he usually did. As previously mentioned, there were lines coming from everywhere, there were monitors all over, and he was full of fluid. His hands and feet were still not a normal color, and they were puffy from all of the fluid. So, I talked them through what they were about to see before they walked in. I said something like this,

"When you walk in, Paul will look very sick. They have added nearly 40lbs of fluid onto him so he looks very puffy. He is on a ventilator, so there is a tube coming out of his mouth and one down his throat. He needs a lot of medicine, so you will see a lot of IVs – sixteen actually. Plus, they just started dialysis, so you will see a many bags of fluid for that machine. There are also a lot of monitors, and they are often alarming because something needs to be checked or changed.

Here is the good news. He made it through the first twenty-four hours. His blood pressure is stabilizing, so he needs a little less help. He still needs a lot of it, but less than before. He is still in very critical condition, but at least now there is more hope. And, all we are focusing on is that hope. Please know, this will not be easy – I just want to try to prepare you before you walk in."

While this wasn't easy for me to do, it seemed to help most of them get a little more prepared. Looking back now, I think this was God's way of helping keep the focus on the positive. Without that conversation, they would only see Paul's survival as nearly impossible. With that conversation, they might at least see the possibility. They were able to hold onto some small bit of hope; the hope that Paul would survive this.

Many of them still broke down when they saw Paul because it was such a sad sight to see. One of the strongest men they knew was lying in a hospital bed fighting for his life. Saying it was emotional would definitely be an understatement.

Here was the mid-afternoon post:

Saturday, February 21st, 2:22pm:
UPDATE: Paul is still resting comfortably. That is my new way of saying sedated. When I spoke to him earlier, he moved his eyebrows and tried to blink. I know he is in there and he can hear me. But, we need him to rest so his body can heal.

Kidneys - dialysis is seeming to work. His creatinine is lower. He is still a little too acidic, but that is also moving in the right direction. They are also removing all of the fluid they are putting in which is good news. I promised him no pictures so I will not post any.

Lungs - he is back down to 65% oxygen. His blood oxygen level was back up to 99%. They will try to get him down to 50% before lowering the PEEP (the pressure to fill his lungs)

Cultures - blood cultures haven't shown anything. Infectious disease doctor says it's because the toxins made by the bacteria were the cause of this - not the bacteria itself. He is going to do another type of test to see if they can find more out.

Liver - still no good news there. But, it doesn't seem to have gotten worse.

Skin - his skin is our next challenge. It is starting to slough off where the rashes were. That causes two potential problems - infection and blood pressure challenges (because of the fluid loss).

> Which brings me to the better news for the day. He was on four pressors to keep his BP up. He is completely off of one and down to about half of another. That is good news both for his heart and so that if he needs help, we have options.
>
> I'm holding his hand and telling him all about your love, prayers & support. Please keep it up! We still need them.

We spent the rest of the afternoon between Paul's room and the ICU waiting room. Paul had lots of visitors. Between visitors, we would take shifts so that Paul was never alone, and everyone could get a little sleep and eat something. While no one really wanted to leave the room, the nurses and staff were concerned for our health, too. They knew this was going to be a long road, or at least hoped for a long road because, again, that meant he was alive. And, if that were the case, we all needed to be strong to help him through it.

It was also about this time I realized how important it was to keep the posts focused on the positive improvements with Paul, and the specific prayer requests that we needed – just as I was doing for those coming to see Paul in the hospital. I didn't want to have people feeling sorry for us, we needed them to be praying for help and healing. For example, I could have written – *"Paul is in a medically-induced coma on life support"*. Writing those words, even now, are hard to write and see. My heart breaks to think of my husband that way. But, that was the reality. He was in a medically induced coma. He was given enough sedation and pain medicines to ensure he stayed asleep and wasn't able to communicate with us. I don't know if that fits the technical term of "medically-induced coma"; however, he was definitely not able to communicate with us, and he needed the ventilator to breathe. If they had removed the ventilator, he would have died.

We needed to stay positive both in the room and in what we wrote to others about Paul's condition. We needed everyone to focus on the positive and to keep praying!

The next time I stepped out of Paul's room, I added this update:

> **Saturday, February 21st, 5:39pm:**
> UPDATE: Paul is still resting comfortably.
>
> BP: His BP is holding strong and is now only on two BP meds. They will start to lower another one slowly to see what he can handle. They are going slow which is good for me.
>
> Lungs: he is down to needing only 60% oxygen with his oxygen level staying around 97. Talked with pulmonology resident and learned a lot about the numbers on the screen. So far, those look good. Goal is to get oxygen needs down to 50% before dropping the PEEP (pressure). It's at 14. They don't like to go above 18, so it's pretty high. Goal there would be down to 5.
>
> Temp: holding at 99.7 without any meds. That is good because they really don't want to add any additional medicines.
>
> Next Update - they are currently doing an ultrasound of all of his organs. That information will be sent to a radiologist to read. Will be a while for that report to come.
>
> Overall, we have seen some positive steps today. This will be a many week / several month process, but our focus is on getting him better and bringing him home.

The abdominal ultrasound was ordered to see if they could find a source for the infection. They wanted to see if there were any pockets of fluid or specific signs of infection in any organs. While they would have rather taken him down for a CT, his condition was too critical to move him. So, this was their next best option. The results of the ultrasound would help them determine the most appropriate next steps.

As I was finishing the last post, I realized I had not written about the conversation with the kids. I wanted to share what we were telling the kids to help our neighbors and friends understand what our kids knew – and more importantly, what they didn't. Here was that post:

> **Saturday, February 21st, 5:46pm:**
> KIDS: I also had the opportunity to go home & see the kids today. To my friend who took the time to talk me through this today - thank you for your guidance & support with this.
>
> Noah & Sarah know that daddy is still sick, but he is at the place where people go to try to get better. That the doctors are doing their best and daddy can use their prayers. Noah did ask how long until daddy can come home and I told him I'm not sure. I don't want to promise something I can't guarantee. And, while I fully believe Paul is coming home with me, I want to be very cautious about making that promise to our kids.
>
> Paulie was a little different story. I talked with him one-on-one to let him know that daddy was really sick and needed lots of prayers. He knows that it will be quite some time before daddy could get better. He also knows that some kids at school might ask him - and just to remember that means their family is praying for daddy, too.
>
> We will need to work on what our new normal will be for them. And, thank you all for your offer to help/support. I'm not sure what that looks like today, but I know we're going to need it.

After I wrote that post, I was back in Paul's room. I sat with him for a little over an hour before the next shift change. I held his hand and talked to him. I told him what had happened that day and the conversation with the kids. While he couldn't respond, I thought it was important to let him know the kids were covered. He just needed to rest and get better.

Saturday, February 21, 2015: ~7:00pm

It was shift change time again, so we all needed to leave Paul's room. We went into the ICU waiting room and had been talking for a little while when I looked up and saw our Parish Priest. He had received the message from the evening before and wanted to ensure he was there to see what he could do for Paul and our family. Prior to coming to the waiting room, he had been in Paul's room praying with him and anointing him with the "Oil of the Sick" – this would be the second time Paul had received his "Last Rites". Our Priest then came to pray with us.

I was sitting on the ICU couch, which had already become my new bed, my home away from home. When I saw Father coming into our corner of the ICU, my eyes welled up with tears. I explained to the family who he was, and welcomed him over to join us. He greeted each person and came over to me. As he knelt by the end of my couch, he asked what I needed. I took a deep breath and prayed for God to help me find the right words; for God to hear my heart and provide me with the words to describe what it was that I needed. Here was what I said,

"I need Paul to get better. I know that God always had a plan and I know that His plan is always good. That said, I need to ensure His plan is to heal Paul and to let him walk out of the hospital with me, going home to take care of our babies. And, if that is not God's plan, I need Him to change that plan. I need that to be His new plan. And, I need you to pray for that. I need God's plan to be that Paul will be healed and coming home with me to take care of our babies. That is what I need."

Our Priest had just been in the room with Paul. He saw what everyone else saw. He saw the monitors, the medicines, the ventilator, the dialysis machine, and my husband lying there, puffed up with significant fluid all over his body. He saw a man that was knocking on death's door. I'm not sure he knew what to say. Truly, I can't blame him. Just as I was very careful not to promise anything to our kids, he was likely being just as careful not to promise anything to me.

He prayed with me for a few minutes and then gathered our families together in prayer. He asked for God to heal Paul and asked for God to be there for each of us. He promised that either he or the Parish Deacon would be back to visit with us and Paul would be added to the prayer list at church. If we needed anything, he wanted us to please give them a call. They were there for us, too.

He went to visit a couple additional parishioners in the hospital before returning to say his good-byes for the night. He spent a few extra moments with several family members before leaving for the evening. I thanked him for his time and his prayers, and then I went back into Paul's room for a while.

Here was my next post:

Saturday, February 21st, 10:54pm:
UPDATE: Paul has had a good day today. The goal today was to stay stable. He did better than that.

BP - down to 2 pressors from 4 with a stable BP. They will slowly titrate another one down and help Paul do the work.

Oxygen - vent is down to 55%. PEEP still at 14.

They are moving him to an "air bed" to help give more air to the wound. They will lift his sheet up, pull one bed out & push the new one in place and then lower him down. Because of that, they didn't want to move anything until he is settled in his new bed.

> They will pull more labs soon. Those results and ultrasound results should be here in the morning.
>
> Goal is to get him settled & keep stable (critical but stable) through the night. Praying for that.
>
> Thank you all for your prayers! While we are not out of the woods, each day gets us closer.

While I didn't want to leave Paul's room, the nurses convinced me that I needed to get some sleep. While they would have preferred I went home to get really good sleep, they knew that I would not be leaving the hospital. So, the ICU waiting room was good enough. They wanted me to rest so that I could be at my best for what was to come. Paul had made it through the first forty-eight hours. Not many, if any, believed he would make it this far. He had a chance to survive, and I needed to be at my best to get him through it. That meant – I needed to get some sleep. So, off to the waiting room I went.

It was that night that I reached into my computer bag and pulled out the book from the Soul Spa Retreat, _Soul Keeping_. I rolled over on the couch, turned my Christian music on low, grabbed my book and settled into a few hours fully focused on God. While He had been here with us the entire time, my focus had been on so very many things. I knew I needed to spend time, some alone time, some quiet time with Him.

Sunday, February 22, 2015

While reading my book and listening to music, I was able to doze off to sleep. It was now the start of day four in the hospital, and we definitely had more than the two people allowed to have spending the night. Paul's parents were there. Both of his sisters and one of my sisters were there with a couple of our brother-in-laws. So, while it sounds like there were lots of people around, I still felt very alone. As I laid on the couch reading and listening to music, I felt as if I was by myself. I know that sounds crazy as we had a hospital waiting room full of family. But, it was just how I felt. My person, my love, my partner was lying in a hospital bed – unable to communicate. I needed our family and friends to stay positive and prayerful. And, I needed God to make His plan be the healing of Paul...

The Complete Healing of Paul

At some point, I drifted off to sleep. While I felt alone around others, I knew God was with me. I could feel His love and strength. That was the only way I could stand. That was the only way I could breathe. That was the only way I was able to allow myself to sleep. I knew that God had this – He always had this – and He would be there with Paul. It was time for me to rest.

Chapter 9: Keeping It Real

Sunday, February 22, 2015

Just like the morning prior, I shot up and was worried about what might have happened during the night. I ran into Paul's room around 6:00am and asked the nurse for the update and spent as much time in his room as I could before shift-change. Here was my update:

> **Sunday, February 22nd, 9:39am:**
>
> UPDATE: Paul made more improvements last night. Here are some of the numbers:
>
> BP - He is down to only 2 BP meds and the 2nd one is half of what it was last night. They will pull both of those off together, so the goal today is getting him off those and allowing his body to do this work.
>
> Kidneys - The dialysis has helped the pH in his blood. He is no longer considered acidotic & his creatinine is down to 5.01- Praise God!
>
> Liver - Those numbers, while still not good, are also improving.
>
> Lungs - He is down to 50% oxygen with PEEP still at 14 and blood gases look good. They will start to lower that PEEP today and see if we can get to the goal of 30% with PEEP below 5 in the next few days
>
> Rash - His rash looks like it is getting better. There is still open skin that is weeping, so we need to keep an eye on that both for infections and pressure, but God answered those specific prayers.

New Concerns:
Platelets - his platelets are really low. This is concerning because that is how he would clot if there is an active bleed. While they don't see any active bleeds right now, they are making decisions on what to do about that

Ultrasound Results - there is an abscess in his abdomen with fluid. They would really like to get a CT Scan to see more before making any decisions, but he is not stable enough to get that. And, since the antibiotics seems to be working, they are likely going to wait another day or so to get that done.

Paul is in there. When I was talking with him this morning, he was moving his eyebrows and moving his thumb. I am trying to help him understand that his body still works, but the medicines are slowing his ability to move it. I know he is scared and I continue to try to talk with him through the process. To let him know the next steps, what is happening, and that we are all here - both in person, and all around the world, praying for him.

Please continue to pray! I don't know if I have said this in the past, but Paul is still on life support. Without all of the interventions right now, he would not be here. So, while I talk about the improvements, because that keeps us positive, he is nowhere near out of the woods yet. This will be a weeks - months process. The good news about that is - just yesterday - we were talking about getting through minutes & hours. We weren't talking about longer-term plans and complications because we didn't know we would have that much time. Your prayers are working. Please know how much we all appreciate them. And, we will keep you updated.

Much Love & Many thanks to everyone!!!

There it was. I finally said it, out-loud, to everyone. Paul was on life-support. Without the ventilator, Paul would not be alive. He had made it to day four in the hospital, but we knew he still had a long road ahead (again, at least we hoped and prayed that to be true). And, if he didn't make it much further, we would have difficult decisions to make. More specifically, I would have some difficult decisions to make. That ventilator was keeping him alive. If he didn't improve, I would need to make the decision to keep him on it, or stop it entirely – to basically "pull the plug" on my husband. While God did not allow my mind to dwell on that circumstance for very long, I did realize that was a very possible scenario. I am so thankful God continued to move my thoughts to Paul's healing instead of the potential negative outcomes. I don't think I would have dealt well with the situation without His continual shifting of my focus to healing and positives versus a very real alternative of negatives and finality.

ICU Photo #1
In a prior post, I mentioned no photos. And, I believed that there were no photos of Paul in the hospital. Much later, I learned that a couple of people took photos of Paul, believing that I would want to see them later. I am glad they did, and I am glad they waited to tell me – as I cannot imagine how I would have reacted.

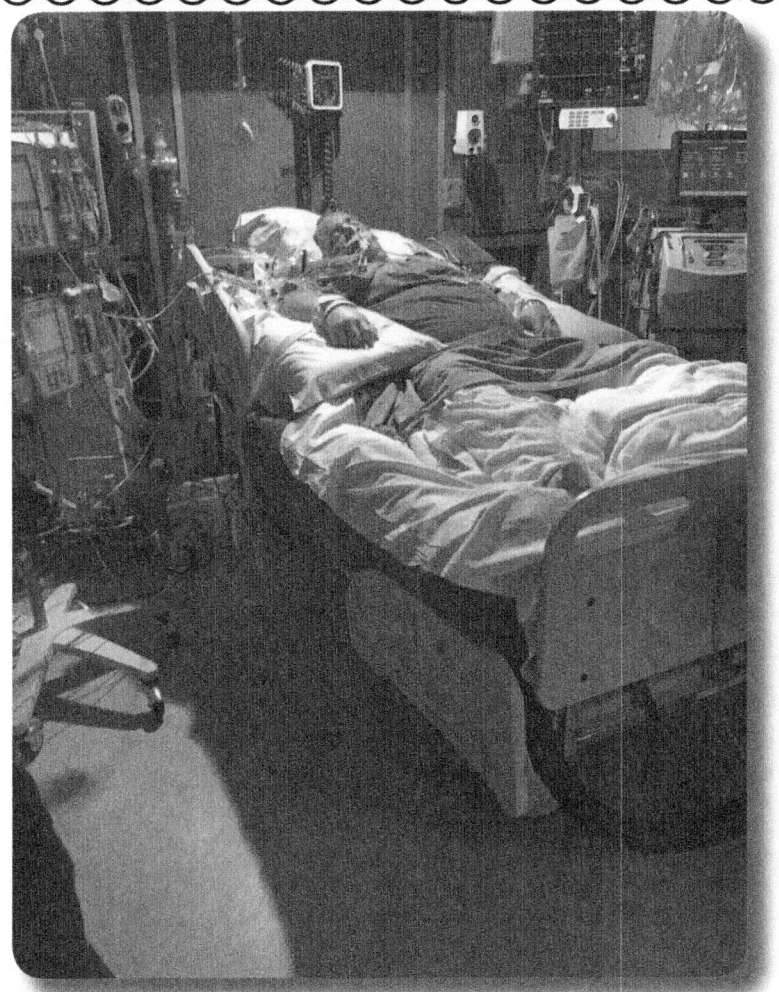

Sunday, February 22nd, ~1:00pm – You can see the ventilator machine in the back left, covered a bit by the IV poles. You can see just how puffy the fluids had made Paul. You can see the lines going into him – IVs, ventilator, NG tube, OG tube. On the right, you can see the monitor we had been watching with his blood pressure and MAP (finally above 65!). To the very right, you can see the dialysis machine.

> *It wasn't easy for me to see this photo. It took me right back to that place; that broken, prayerful, hopeful, and struggling place. Knowing that I needed to be strong, and not knowing where my next breath would come from, or how I would be able to put one foot in front of the other. I also struggled with whether or not to include this photo. I decided to add it because I felt like God ensured that we had the picture. This would help people reading this get a glimpse into just how bad things were.*

I spent the rest of the afternoon in Paul's room, talking with him and talking with friends and family who were able to visit. As I did the day prior, I took on the responsibility of preparing each person for what they were about to see when they saw Paul lying in the hospital bed. While it still wasn't an easy thing to do, I felt that it was best for them to see the improvements instead of the visual they were about to see. Paul was definitely improving. He was still not "out of the woods"...not by a long shot. But, he had made it to day four, and he had a chance. I needed everyone to focus on that chance. This was my next post during evening shift-change:

Sunday, February 22nd, 7:57pm:
UPDATE: Today has been a day full of progression.

BP: Paul is down to 4mcg/minute of one pressor & his blood pressure is stable. They will hope to stop that tonight. The goal was to get these down today, and we might be off of all BP help - AMEN! BP is pretty stable at 100/70 and pulse is down to 82.

Kidney: Creatinine was down to 5.01 this morning from 7.5 at it's high. Labs are only pulled once per day, so we will need to wait until tomorrow to see what that looks like. Good news is that once the BP meds are off, they can start pulling off extra fluid via dialysis. The doctor said he has about 20L of extra fluid now, and they will only pull 1-2L per day. So, this will take some time - and they cannot start until we are sure his body can handle it.

Lungs: They have kept him at 50% and the PEEP was down to 8 (from 14). He was tolerating that well and was maintaining at 97 - AMEN! The goal is to get the PEEP down to 5 and then start dropping the oxygen help to 30%.

Skin: The rash on his back is improving which is a true answer to specific prayers. He had other spots of rash around his body, so those are starting to peel / slough like his back. They are watching those and taking care of them when they do.

Paul: He is resting comfortably, and he sometimes makes extra movements to let us know he is in there. He moves eyebrows and squeezes his eyes shut. He hasn't opened his eyes since Friday, but I know he is still in there. He has moved his toes & thumb (for those of you who knew Grandpa Muszik - he definitely gave us the thumb :)). And, when they were moving him the last time, it seemed like he was trying to use his legs to help.

Kids: The kids have been doing well and they have had a house full to keep them busy. This next week will be a true test. While they are used to me traveling for work, their dad is always with them. So, knowing that Paul is here, I am worried about them. Please pray for God to protect their minds & hearts.

Home: Thank you to everyone for your prayers, support and offers to help. We are starting to get the house needs figured out. We will get something out soon, and truly appreciate the offers / willingness to help.

After I sent the post, I closed my computer, sat on the couch, and watched the clock. Shift changes had become increasingly more difficult for me. I wanted to be in there to know what they were saying. I wanted to hear, from their words, what they thought about Paul's chances for survival. I wanted to keep the nurses positive, too! While I was praying for Paul during shift change, I was also praying for the nurses. The nurses were critical to Paul having a positive outcome. The doctors make the decisions, and the nurses put those decisions into action. They were the ones who were with the patient continually during their twelve-hour shifts and contacted the doctors when they saw unexpected outcomes. The nurses were crucial to the patient's successful outcome...to Paul's successful outcome. We had been blessed with amazing nurses. Praise God! And, I wanted to dedicate some specific prayers for them, too.

Shift change was also the time when most of the family gathered to discuss the previous twelve hours. It was a time to connect, discuss what the doctors had said, and to review Paul's progress during the day. Plus, we were all trying to grab a bite to eat, as our meals were no longer at "normal" times. We seemed to find a rhythm of breakfast and dinner during shift change, and lunch was whenever we either needed to be out of the room for a procedure, or a quick few minutes during the day. As people were visiting the hospital, many brought food and snacks for us, which was amazingly helpful and truly appreciated. We were also so very thankful for the meal train. Our family at home had already received the first meal on Saturday and brought the leftovers to the hospital on Sunday for those of us staying there. That meant that both our family at home and our family at the hospital were able to enjoy the great food prepared, with love, from our friends. We will always be forever grateful for that!

So, after having a little to eat, we were preparing to head back into Paul's room for a few hours before it would again be time for us to sleep. Here was my next post:

> **Sunday, February 22nd, 11:00pm:**
> UPDATE: I had to send one additional update tonight. Two things:
>
> 1-the nurse came rushing down to the waiting room before the end of shift change to tell us the new room rules because - Paul is waking up!!!
>
> While we still have a long road, this is great news! He opened his eyes and was moving around. That said, he still has lots of healing to do. He needs to rest to let the meds work and help his body get stronger. So, while I cannot wait to look into his handsome eyes, I need to be patient and let him heal.
>
> That brings me to update #2.
>
> I passed the resident who was with me the first night we were here. He stopped and said - *"your husband - he is a miracle!"* **AMEN!** I thanked him for all they did for Paul. And he said - *"God needs thanks for that!"* I agreed and said *"Yes! And, you all made sure the medicine was on board so God could do the work."*
>
> **PRAISE GOD!**
>
> While I know we still have a long road with ups and downs - progress & setbacks - God continues to provide very clear signs that He is here and He is providing! Hallelujah & AMEN!

Yes, you read that right! The very person who told me to call our family because Paul *"didn't have much time left"*, the person who said, *"I guess he has a chance"*, was now calling my husband,

"A MIRACLE!"

God had provided many miracles in keeping Paul alive. God ensured we got Paul to the hospital *in time* so that these miracles could happen. God helped the doctors make the right decisions, do the right procedures, and get the right medicines on board *in time*. While I never believed God made any of this mess happen, I did believe He would see us through it – and now the doctors were seeing that possibility, too! While Paul was still not out of the woods, there was more than just a small chance he would survive. *Praise God!*

As you can imagine, it had been a very long day. It had been a very long four days. And, we had no idea when this would end or what the outcome would be. The family spent a little time talking that night, but we all were still so very tired. We talked about who would be spending time with Paul during the evening, and then I went to my couch. I again grabbed my book, turned on my music, and spent the time filling my head, my heart, and my soul with God. I needed His strength. I couldn't do this on my own. I was so thankful for everything that He had already done, and I knew we still had a long road. Paul needed Him! We needed Him! I needed Him!

Chapter 10: Reality Setting In

Monday, February 23, 2015

As I woke up on Monday with Paul still "resting comfortably", I was a mix of emotions. I wanted to be home with the kids. I wanted to get Paulie up and onto the bus. I wanted to have something to say to him that would give him hope...hope that his Daddy was going to be okay. I wanted to snuggle on our itty bittys and tell them great news. But, there wasn't great news to share; at least not any positive news that they would understand. If I were to share with them some of their Daddy's progress, it would mean also sharing just how bad the situation was for him. *Not yet. It wasn't time yet.*

With red, swollen eyes, I went into Paul's room to get the update from the nurse. She gave me the news and I sat with Paul for a while. While the news was good, all of this started to hit me. *How long will we be here? Will Paul be coming home with us? While I believed he would be, was that really God's plan? And, when he does wake up, what were the long-term effects of this terrible infection?*

In talking with other people, I guess this was normal. When your focus moves from counting each minute because it might be your last over to hoping for survival and long-term effects, there is a wave of emotion that hits you. It's both the realization that imminent death is no longer the concern (which is a rush of positive emotions) and the realization that there is still such a long road ahead with no way of knowing how long or what the final outcome will be (which is a rush of anxiety and stress). And, at some point, you need to let it out. I wasn't fully ready to let it out, but I could feel it coming.

So, I left Paul's room for shift change and sent an email to Paulie's teacher. She was an amazing young woman. She, along with his two previous teachers, had helped Paulie have a true love of learning. They brought out the best in him. He loves reading, writing, STEM – really, all of it. We are truly blessed to have amazing teachers in our school system (and in the Lutheran Preschool he attended). I need to tell them that!

Anyway, I sent her a note to let her know that Paulie would be back in school that day. I let her know what we shared with Paulie, so she knew what to say. I asked her to please let me know how he was doing in school, and if there was anything she needed from me to please give me a call. I also asked her to keep her same expectations of Paulie. I know he was going through a tough time, but I didn't want him to "get away with things" he wouldn't usually get away with. I didn't want him to even try it (and I assumed he wouldn't). He is such a good kid; I just didn't want this to be the start of a potential downward slide. She had sent a couple of e-mails over the weekend checking in on Paul. She had offered to do anything she could to help. I ended the note thanking her for her offer, and specifically for her prayers for Paul. He needed them.

After that, I left the hospital and went home. I wanted to be there in the morning to take Paulie to school. I wanted to see him and answer any questions he had about what was going on. I wanted to see his eyes and know that he was okay. Well, at least as okay as he could be considering the situation.

I got home around 8:00am. Paulie was up and ready for school. He was finishing his breakfast when I arrived. I sat with him for a few minutes before running upstairs for a quick shower. It had been an emotional morning and I wanted to be my best for Paulie. I knew I would come back to see the itty bittys, but I didn't quite know how Paulie was feeling or what he was thinking.

When I came back downstairs, I sat with Paulie for a while playing games and watching TV. Soon, it was time to leave for school. I wanted to leave a little early, that would give us time to talk in the car. It would just be the two of us, and I could answer any questions he had.

In the car, I reminded Paulie of our talk on Saturday. I told him that kids may or may not ask about his Daddy. Either way, I wanted him to be prepared to answer questions and wanted to know what questions he had for me. It was then that he asked, *"Mom, does Dad have his cell phone with him?"*

I replied, *"No, Paulie. They are keeping Daddy very well rested. He is not allowed to have his cell phone. I think his phone is here with me in my purse. Why do you ask, buddy?"*

He said, *"I have been playing Dad in Trivia Crack, and a couple of games have expired now. He hasn't been playing me, and Dad always plays me."*

My eyes filled with tears as I thought of our little Paulie trying to play the games with his Daddy and not knowing why his Daddy wasn't playing back. What must have been going through his mind? And, Thank God he was willing to ask the question!

I smiled in the mirror at him and repeated, *"Daddy doesn't have his cell phone, Buddy. And, thank you for asking me that question. Is there anything else on your mind? Do you have any other questions for me or about your Daddy?"*

Paulie said he didn't, and we had arrived at school. I pulled up and opened the van door for Paulie to head into school. I said, *"Paulie, we love you and we are all so very proud of you. You are a great kid! I hope you have a really great day! If you need anything, let your teacher know and she will get in touch with me. And, keep praying, Buddy. Daddy needs all the prayers he can get."*

As I drove back home, I thought of just how much that little boy had been dealing with. *What other questions might be on his mind? How could I help him?* And, just how overwhelmingly thankful I was that he asked me that question about his Dad having his cell phone. I was so glad I was able to answer that one for him so that he wasn't continuing to wonder.

When I arrived back home, our itty bittys were awake. We spent some time snuggling and watching TV. Noah asked how his Daddy was doing and how long I was going to be able to stay home. I told him that his Daddy was getting better but still needed lots of prayers. I would be going back to the hospital very soon to be with Daddy. Then, he asked when his Daddy would be coming home. In our house, we usually describe the time until an event by the number of sleeps. So, hearing Noah's question, Sarah added, *"Yeah, Mommy. How many sleeps until Daddy comes home?"* I obviously didn't have an answer to that question. I let them know that their Daddy was continuing to get better, but he was still very sick. The doctors were doing all they could do, and so was their Dad. I asked them if they had been praying for their Daddy, and both said they were. I asked them to keep praying; to ask God to completely heal their Daddy and bring him home.

I sat there for a little while longer, but I knew I wanted to get back to the hospital. Plus, I didn't have the answers the kids needed or wanted. I was spent, and I didn't want them to see me break. I ran back upstairs quickly to pack some clean clothes for a few days, and added this morning report:

Monday, February 23rd, 9:11am:

UPDATE: Paul had another good night!

BP: his BP is 112/75 and holding on its own - all pressors are off!! Praise God!

Kidneys: Creatinine down to 4.5. Still no urine. They will start pulling 50mL/hr. If he tolerates that, they will go up to 100mL/hr.

Lungs: the pulmonologist hasn't been in yet. We believe he will start dropping the PEEP down and then the oxygen. They kept that stable last night as they worked on the BP.

Skin: his rashes seem to be improving. I read a lot of skin might slough off - even in places where the rash wasn't.

> Things to watch:
>
> Platelets: his platelets continue to go down slowly. They are down to 31. They really should be above 150. Please pray that Paul's platelet count increases and he has no active bleeds while they are rising
>
> Paul: I still haven't seen his eyes. I have seen him "wake up" and he is very agitated. I would be too with all of these lines, machines, and especially the tubes in his nose & mouth. That said, I know he is in there & he is coming back to us
>
> Please continue your prayers! Today, we need platelets to rise, no active bleeds, and Paul to tolerate the dialysis pull to help his kidneys turn back on.
>
> God is moving mountains and you are all helping! We cannot thank you enough!!

While I believed every word of this post, I also had this overwhelming amount of emotions. But, it wasn't time to let them out. God was moving mountains! No one believed Paul would live this long. Everyone believed he would have died on Friday or Saturday. But, it was Monday and he was still alive. Not only was he alive; he was continuing to show small improvements each and every day. We had to keep our focus on that. We needed to be thankful and prayerful.

And, I needed to be positive, prayerful, thankful and strong for our kids. I needed to be that for everyone at the hospital and everyone at our house. I needed to be that for everyone who was praying for us. I didn't have time to break. It wasn't time. I needed to be strong – and I needed God for that. So, I sat upstairs and prayed. I needed a few quiet minutes with God. I was truly thankful for all He had already done. And, there was still more work Paul needed, I needed, we all needed Him to do.

While I wanted to stay at home for a while, I also knew I needed to get back to the hospital. I wanted to be there with Paul, and I didn't want to miss the rounding doctors. So, I grabbed my bag, gave the itty bittys an extra snuggle, and went back to the hospital.

When I arrived back at the hospital, I could see the worry in our family's eyes. While the morning report was overall positive, Paul's mid-morning to afternoon was not so positive. Paul's sedation and pain meds were not keeping him calm, and he was not making it easy to get him comfortable. We had heard that, in the ICU, there would likely be positives along with setbacks. We had been blessed with only focusing on the positives for his first four days in the ICU. We were on day five, and we were experiencing one of those setback days. Here was the update:

Monday, February 23rd, ~7pm (edited on 2/25):
UPDATE: I guess this is what they mean when they say we will hit a few "bumps" in the road.

Kidneys - Dialysis was working and they were pulling 50mL per hour additional fluid off of Paul. Then, the dialysis machine clotted.

Lungs - Because they were moving Paul and he was agitated, they upped his oxygen to 100% while keeping PEEP at 5.

So - our two goals today: lowering the vent and drawing more fluid from dialysis were moving in the right direction until this afternoon.

I guess tonight's goal will be to get Paul back to where he was this morning. Please pray the night will be good. Please pray we can all get some sleep - we need it! Please pray we are able to help move Paul back in a positive direction.

That post wasn't originally written that way; I made significant edits a little while after I posted it. Remember when I said I was a bottle of emotions. I was like a boiling teapot ready to blow. And, this was also the day that Paul was experiencing a setback. So, my original post was full of much of that emotion, in a very negative mindset, focused on the setbacks and "who" was to blame. I blamed the nurses, the hospital, the doctors, etc. I had a lot of blame to go around. Looking back now, I think the truth of the matter was that I was scared. I just came to grips with us not needing to worry about every minute, and I was fearful we were going back there. I was hopeful that we would soon be able to have Paul wake up and talk with the kids. I was so afraid that wouldn't happen now. My mind went to the very negative what-ifs, and I posted that.

I am truly sorry for that post. You will see my written response to everyone on February 25th at 12:22am. But, before I get to that, here was the evening update with minor edits:

Monday, February 23rd, 9:19pm:

UPDATE: Praising God!!!

Thank you for all of you who lifted up prayers for Paul! He:
- Had a bath
- Is resting comfortably
- Has ventilator back down to 55 Oxygen / 5 PEEP
- Has dialysis machine back on - pulling even. They will work on pulling the 50 throughout the night depending on his pressure (right now looks good)
- Peed - YEAH!!! This is great news!
- Pooped

Thank you all for praying and Praise God for answering!

Praying all is good, we all get a good night sleep, Paul continues to improve, and I can send update with numbers in the morning.

> And, please know how much your comments, notes, texts, e-mails mean to all of us! While I cannot answer them all, please know I do read them all. The only way we are staying strong is by the grace of God and the energy from all of you! Truly - thank you!

I had asked for everyone to pray for improvements, they did, and God ensured we had what we needed. I am still so very sorry for what I wrote. It wasn't reality. It was just all of the emotion, the anxiety, the fear coming out – and I focused all of that in the very wrong direction.

To add to that, earlier that afternoon, I placed a call to the Human Resources department to start the paperwork for Family Medical Leave Act (FMLA). I thought I would be able to take both caregiver time and my vacation time. With both of those, I would have five weeks to figure things out. Unfortunately, I learned that it doesn't work that way. While I would be able to send in the paperwork for FMLA, by law, I would only be able to use the vacation days I had accrued thus far during the year. So, after only eight days of caregiver leave and vacation, I would need to start on unpaid leave.

Considering Paul was a stay-at-home dad and the only income we had was mine, I was devastated. On top of whatever we would owe for hospital bills, I also needed to think about how we would pay our regular monthly bills. *What would we do?* There was just so much to think about, to worry about, to pray about. And, while I thought I was giving that stress and worry to God, I truly wasn't. I was holding onto it. I needed to figure it out. God was ready with an answer, but I wasn't patiently waiting for it. I was trying to take control of a situation I had no control over. I needed to let go. So, I grabbed my book, turned on my music, and curled up on my couch for the night. Before I jumped into my book, my sister reminded me to read my daily devotional from Sarah Young's <u>*Jesus Calling*</u>.

I have the app on my phone, so I opened it and read the message for the day. Here is a the message for February 23rd:

"Be on guard against the pit of self-pity. When you are weary or unwell, this demonic trap is the greatest danger you face. Don't even go near the edge of the pit. It's edges crumble easily, and before you know it, you are on the way down. It is ever so much harder to get out of the pit than to keep safe distance from it. That is why I tell you to be on guard.

There are several ways to protect yourself from self-pity. When you are occupied with praising and thanking Me, it is impossible to feel sorry for yourself. Also, the closer you live to Me, the more distance there is between you and the pit. Live in the Light of My Presence by fixing your eyes on Me. Then you will be able to run with endurance the race that is set before you, without stumbling or falling."

What I have found through reading <u>Jesus Calling</u>, the message is always perfectly timed. And, I do mean ALWAYS! I was so thankful for this reminder. Even on a day that seemed to include several big setbacks, I was to focus on God. I was to be thankful for all He had already provided, and pray for the needs for that day and the next. One day at a time, one breath at a time. I needed to focus on Him.

I rolled over with tear-filled eyes, so thankful for all that God had already provided. That said, it was still such a long road with no end in sight. Not only no end, but no understanding of what we would find when we reached the destination either. So, I prayed deeper and harder than I had ever prayed. I asked God to help me keep my eyes on Him and Him alone. I asked Him to please protect my heart and mind. I wanted to only see what He wanted me to see, focus on what He wanted me to focus on. I thanked Him for all He had done thus far, and begged for Paul's complete healing.

Chapter 11: Hold It Together – No Time for a Breakdown!

Tuesday, February 24, 2015

I woke up on Tuesday with a partial plan. While I was still very emotional and overwhelmed, I knew God had a plan for us, and He would see us through this. It was my job to be thankful and focused on what He wanted me to see.

Before doing anything else, I wanted to see Paul and get the information on his night before the next shift change. Here was what I learned:

> **Tuesday, February 24th, ~7am (edited on 2/25):**
>
> UPDATE: Paul had a really good night! Praise God!
>
> Kidneys: Paul has made more urine. His creatinine is down to 4.33. They said the decrease will now potentially go slower. The dialysis is pulling 50mL/hr and we will look to increase that to 100mL/hr today. That will help pull off the additional fluid.
>
> Lungs: He is at 55% oxygen / 5 PEEP. With that, his oxygen saturation is steady around 92-93. They are pulling a blood gas to ensure his organs are getting the oxygen (which they should be, but I am glad they are checking). Goal here would be to get down to 30% / 5 - but that might not be today. He cannot get off of the vent until we get to those numbers. He will also get a chest x-ray today just to ensure his lungs are still looking good. Praying for that!
>
> Platelets: His platelets have gone up to 33. While they are still low, they have stopped the downward trend! Praise God for that specific answer to prayers!

> White Count: His white count is a little elevated which can be signs of his body fighting an infection. The doctor believes it is more likely due to the steroids as he is on three major antibiotics.
>
> Abscess: They are also not worrying about the abscess yet. The challenge is that they would like to do a CT with contrast, but his kidneys cannot handle that right now. Since he is on those antibiotics, they are okay to wait until they can get him down for a CT.
>
> Goals for today:
> Kidneys - making urine & they can pull 100mL/hr from dialysis
> Lungs - x-ray shows good lungs, Vent can be brought down
> Platelets - continue to rise
>
> Thank you all for your prayers! He is getting better and you are all helping him and us through the process! Truly, thank you! And - Praise God for all this progress!

Truly, Praise God for all of those improvements, and for the specific things to focus on and pray for! As we lifted up Paul in prayer and asked for very specific outcomes, God was providing. He was helping us see – He was helping everyone see – He had this all under control. God was not overwhelmed. He had this. We just needed to be faithful and patient. This was going to be a long journey, and our eyes needed to stay fixed on Him.

As I mentioned, when I woke up that morning, I had a partial plan. I knew we were going to need money to pay some bills, and I had been worried about where we would find that money. Since we had been concerned about my job for some time, we had become pretty good with our finances. We paid off both cars. We were able to pay off anything we put on the credit cards each month. While we didn't have much in the way of liquid cash, I knew that we had some money available in stocks and stock options. Even if they weren't at the best time to cash in, that money was needed to help us get through this time. So, after seeing Paul, I logged into our financial website and sold off what was available. Interestingly, the total amount available was almost exactly three months worth of my salary. As I clicked the button to sell the stock and options, I was so very thankful for the financial situation we were in. I thanked God for helping us get there; for helping us prepare for any situation we would find ourselves in. I thanked Him for helping me to remember that option, so that I could stop worrying about money and keep my focus on Him and on Paul.

One would think that the answer to that prayer would help me calm down. Unfortunately, the very opposite was true. It was then that I started to break. I felt as if I couldn't hold it in any longer. While I had that answer, I really wanted more answers. I felt so very alone. While there were always people around, my rock was lying in bed – unable to communicate. And, while he seemed to be getting back on track, *would we experience other setbacks? Would we have more days like Monday? How much longer would I need to wait to see his amazing eyes? How much longer until I could hold his hand and he would hold mine back? How much longer until I would hear him say that he loved me? How much longer would I need to be strong? How much longer?*

I am still amazed at how I pulled myself together to write this evening update:

Tuesday, February 24th, 8:19pm:
UPDATE: Paul has had a great afternoon!

Kidneys - They were able to continue to pull an extra 50mL/hr all day - Hallelujah!

> We are hoping that, if Paul can handle it, they will be able to up that tomorrow to 100mL/hr. He still isn't producing much urine - please pray that he starts peeing soon!
> This is kind of funny as my sister is working on potty training Sarah this week. We are praying for pee from both Daddy & Sarah!
>
> Lungs - Paul still fights the vent when he wakes up. He bites down a bit and coughs a lot. Today, they changed his meds so he was calmer most of the day - which was a true answer to prayers! They were able to drop his oxygen needs - his PEEP is up a bit to 8. Praying for a good night so they may be able to work on that, too.
>
> Rash - his rash is really getting better! Praise God for answering that specific prayer!
>
> Paul - I remember when Sarah was in the NICU, she was on "low stimulation." That meant - low lights, low voices, minimal / no touch. While her lungs were healing, we needed to give her time to heal. With Paul, he has been so sedated that hasn't been an issue. Now that he is waking up more, we need to transition to "low stimulation". I sat in his room most of the day and just watched him. He is so amazingly handsome! I just love that man so very much.
>
> They are in the middle of shift change, so I will head back in soon. I will see if there are any specific prayers for tonight and add them all to the final report. More to come soon...

I went back into his room and spoke with the evening nurse. She had been a nurse who had been with Paul before, so I knew she had this covered. And, I knew I needed to get out of the hospital. I needed to go back home. Our kids would already be in bed, but that would give me time to talk with my sister. I just needed to breathe.

I told Paul's parents I was leaving for the night. I knew I had to be back by 6:30am, as the next day was a "Dad's Breakfast" at Paulie's school. Yep, that's right. The next morning, all of the first graders would invite their dads to school for a special breakfast. And, Paulie's Daddy was still lying in a bed, in a medically induced coma, on life-support. He couldn't even talk with his Dad. Oh, how that broke my heart.

Paul's dad had asked if he could go with Paulie. When I asked Paulie if that would be okay, he was really excited to have his Papa come to school with him. Earlier in the year, my dad was able to spend some time with Paulie at school for "Grandparents" day, which was a lot of fun. He was excited to be able to introduce his other grandfather to his classmates. That said, we only had one car at the hospital, so I would need to be back in time for Paul's dad to drive back to the house to take Paulie to school. We made those arrangements, and I left.

That felt like the longest drive home. While I wasn't yet breaking down, I couldn't stop the tears from rolling out of my eyes. It was like a continual stream. And, when I arrived at home, I fell into my sister's arms. I just needed someone to hold me. While she couldn't tell me it would be okay, she could tell me that God was in control.

It was then that I finally said this out loud.

"What if Paul doesn't wake up? I know God is good. I know His greatness is not wrapped up in this outcome. And, I know He has a plan for Paul. But, what if that plan isn't full healing? What if that plan isn't for him to come home with me? What if he never comes back to this house? What if he never sleeps next to me in this bed? Please pray with me. Please pray for God to have that plan. Please pray God will bring him home with me. Please pray for complete healing."

Tammy held me, and we prayed. We prayed for God to have the plan to heal Paul. We prayed for complete healing. We prayed for God to provide His peace beyond understanding and to provide His strength. We thanked Him for all He had already provided, and asked Him to finish the work He had started. And, if that was not His plan, we asked Him to change it.

I also asked my sister to specifically pray for Paul's spirit. When he woke up, I was worried about how this experience would effect his view on God. I asked my sister to pray with me that Paul would wake up with a thankful spirit. That he would be seeking an even deeper, more personal relationship with Jesus. While it wasn't time to ask everyone to pray for that because there were still other prayers we needed answered first, I wanted both she and I to continue to specifically pray for his spirit.

After all of that, I was emotionally spent. That said, I also knew I wanted to update the previous posts, and to write an apology to all those who read them. Those posts did not reflect the person I wanted to be. So, I went down to our couch (I couldn't sleep in my bed without Paul there) and I wrote the following post:

> **Wednesday, February 25th, 12:22am:**
> UPDATE: Paul had a really great afternoon. I saw him for a short time after shift change and then came home to sleep. The reason - I am truly disappointed in myself.
>
> The purpose of this blog and writing about this journey is to lift Paul up in prayer to God, to engage all of you amazing prayer warriors in praying for specific goals, and glorifying God for all of the miracles He is providing. You have all been AMAZING and God is Moving Mountains!!
>
> That said, I failed. I failed because in my tired, stressed, overwhelmed state of mind, I used this blog to vent. To vent about a situation where I only knew my 50%. And, while I am certain this is not the only time I have failed in this way, I want to apologize to all of you - as that is not the purpose of this blog - AT ALL!

> I have updated my previous post to remove any specific comments. Paul truly has been receiving exceptional care. Minor setbacks are expected. However, he has been moving in a positive direction and I know that everyone is on the same team - getting Paul healthy.
>
> One additional request - please know I am not asking for and am not looking for any support for my actions. I can make every excuse in the world as to why I did it; however, none of those excuses make it right.
>
> I ask for your forgiveness for my failure. I promise to use this blog in a positive way, to share Paul's story and to glorify God for His Amazing Miracles.

With that, I closed the computer, turned on my music, and curled up on my own couch for the night. I knew I would only have a few short hours to sleep before I needed to be back on my way to the hospital. Paulie had a big morning with his Papa, and I needed to make sure that was a great morning for them both. But, before I could fall asleep, I took the time to read the February 24th devotional from *Jesus Calling*. While I won't recite it here, please know that it was absolutely perfect. With that, I rolled over and cried myself to sleep, knowing that God's Love was always enough.

Chapter 12: Two Steps Forward... One Step Back – It's Still Progress

Wednesday, February 25, 2015
I woke up around 5:30am, grabbed my things and headed back to the hospital. I wanted to get there for Paul's dad, and I wanted to check in with the nurse on how Paul did overnight. Here was my morning report:

> **Wednesday, February 25th, 8:16am:**
> UPDATE: I guess I didn't prepare myself for what Paul waking up meant. Paul wakes up like an angry fighter.
>
> Please pray they are able to find the right medicine mix to help him rest and heal. He can't get better when he keeps fighting
>
> Kidneys - Creatinine down to 4.22 (from 4.33). No pee last night. Praying for pee today and the ability to up the dialysis to pull 100.
>
> Lungs - he is fighting the vent. They needed to move him up to 50 oxygen / 8 PEEP. He bites down on the vent which is also concerning because we don't want him to break the tube. And, he is grinding on it. Praying the meds will help him relax and allow him to heal.
>
> Platelets doubled!! From 33 to 66 - HALLELUJAH!
>
> New challenge:
> White count is elevated. They will do a culture to see if something else is growing. With all of the antibiotics, that doesn't seem possible, but I am glad they are checking.
>
> Prayers for today:
> Kidneys - pull more fluid & start peeing

> - Lungs - stop fighting vent so they can reduce his need of it
> - Resting medicine - find the right mix to help him stay calm.
> - White count - the reason for this elevation will be identified and solved quickly.
>
> Thank you for praying! Afternoon update later today.

While writing this post, and for the remainder of the day, tears were continually streaming from my eyes. I couldn't hold it together. I sat in Paul's room, listening to my music, reading my book, going back a few days in <u>Jesus Calling</u> to see what I had missed, and reading my daily Bible verses. I was so very thankful for the opportunity to write out the information on Paul's progress because, looking at him, he still had such a long road. He was still so very puffy. There were still so many IV lines going into his body. While there were less than before, there were still a lot. And, now, he wasn't cooperating with the nurses – the ones who were there to help him. I just needed him to stop that and to please let them do their job. If they couldn't clear his lungs, he could end up with pneumonia. We definitely didn't need that to happen! He needed to cooperate.

That said, they wanted us to stay back from him. They wanted us to continue with the "low stimulation" to try to keep him calm. That was so very hard! I just wanted to hold his hand. I wanted to talk to him. I wanted to crawl in bed with him and have him hold me. I wanted him to wake up. I wanted to see his eyes.

"Dear God, please! Please heal him! I am so thankful for all You have already done. You have moved mountains. You have parted seas. You continue to provide miracles each and every moment. We just need more. I know You know this. Please, hear my heart. Please save my husband. Please!"

Just when I thought I was at my end, Paul's dad arrived back at the hospital. He had spent the morning with Paulie at school and then some time at the house with my sister and our itty bittys. When he got back, he described the morning, and how Paulie was the hit of the show. Each first grader was asked to introduce their dad or special person. Most of the children looked down and quietly introduced themselves and their person. Not Paulie! Paulie grabbed the microphone from the principal (politely), introduced himself and told everyone about his Papa. He shared that they both have the same name, but his Papa wasn't a "senior" because he didn't have a middle name. As he was walking off of the stage, he said, *"Papa, that was funny, wasn't it!"* What a great little man we have! Even in the midst of this most difficult time, he was trying to be as normal as possible – and gave everyone a reason to smile. That was what I needed. If Paulie was able to smile during this, I needed to do the same.

Paulie and his Papa at the 1st Grade "Dad's Breakfast". Look at Paulie holding that microphone and owning that stage! Way to go, Buddy! We Love You!!

Paul had already made so much progress, and I had faith he would continue to improve. God had already provided so many miracles, and I just knew He wasn't done yet. I needed to snap out of it. There would be time to fully breakdown later. Now was not the time.

I went back in the ICU waiting room during shift change and wrote this update:

Wednesday, February 25th, 7:37pm:
UPDATE: Paul is back resting comfortably. They were able to come up with a good mix of medicines that have seemed to help him rest and not get so agitated - Praise God!

Kidneys: Dialysis is working and pulling an extra 50mL/hr. Still hoping to pull more tomorrow to get some of this extra fluid off. Decided not to give the diuretic, as he hasn't peed much more since yesterday.

Lungs: His breathing has improved. He is down to 40 Oxygen / 5 PEEP with saturations around 97-98. Once they get him down to 30 Oxygen / 5 PEEP, they can start to consider pulling the vent. That will likely not be tomorrow, but maybe on Friday. Praying for that.

Paul: We are still needing to keep low stimulation in the room. I was in there much of the day just staring at him. Praising God for the miracle to still have Paul here with us! I know we will have a long road to recovery, but at least we are talking about recovery - AMEN!!

I am not sure we will learn much more, so there may not be an evening report tonight. Here are my prayers for tonight:
- I pray Paul rests comfortably and continues to heal
- I pray we are able to turn the vent down and set a timeline for removal
- I pray we are able to up the dialysis pull to 100mL/hr and are able to get more of this fluid off

> Thank you so very much for your prayer support! More to come tomorrow.

After I wrote the update, I curled up on my ICU couch and rested. I think my body had finally given up. I had been such a ball of emotions all day. I needed to sleep. I needed quiet time to heal. I needed to let God heal my mind and my heart. I needed Him to heal my soul. I needed to be strong; that would only work with God's Strength.

Thursday, February 26, 2015

When I woke up the next morning, I felt almost refreshed. I knew God had this, and I needed to let Him keep it. He was the only One who could heal Paul; I needed to be patient, prayerful, and thankful. I needed to rely on His Strength, and He would see us all through this. And, I still believed Paul would experience the miracle of complete healing.

I went into Paul's room to check in on his night. Here was the update:

> **Thursday, February 26th, 5:47am:**
> UPDATE: Paul had a fairly restful night. He awoke on his own about an hour ago without stimulation and needed more meds.
>
> Kidneys: Creatinine went up a little 4.3 from 4.22. That is the wrong direction. Please pray for his kidneys!
>
> Lungs: he has been stable on 40 oxygen / 5 PEEP. Hoping to drop that down today to possibly think about removing vent on Friday.
>
> Platelets - 91 - Praise God!!!! Still a little low, but nearly triple where they were when they bottomed out.
>
> White Count - still elevated, but lower than yesterday - Hallelujah!

> I will sit with him until 7 to see if any of the attendings come through and determine goals for today.
>
> If there is one specific prayer for today - it's for his kidneys. Please pray they kick back in and start working. They are very resilient organs, so this is possible. Just praying God makes it happen.

As I wrote this post, I kept looking at Paul and could see that he was coming back to us. I wasn't quite sure when he would be fully back, but I just felt like it would be soon. And, while there were a few minor setbacks, he was in such a better place than he was when we got there. Today was Day Eight. **Day Eight!** He wasn't supposed to make it to Day Two! God had brought him this far; He would finish the job. He would provide complete healing. I just knew it.

I was in a much better mood throughout the day. I was able to focus on the positives, the improvements, and the mountains God had already moved. This was perfect timing, as Paul was not having a great day. The day was full of ups and downs. It was truly a roller coaster, but I was ready to handle it.

I had many quiet moments with just Paul and I in his room. I used this time to read the *Jesus Calling* daily devotional and the bible verses for the day. Each of them seemed to be perfectly chosen for our daily needs. A few lines from *Jesus Calling* that were specifically appropriate were:

> *"...Your future looks uncertain and feels flimsy – even precarious. That is how it should be. Secret things belong to the Lord, and future things are secret things. When you try to figure out the future, you are grasping at things that are Mine..."*

Talk about specifically appropriate messaging for exactly what I needed that day – everyday! It filled me up, and I was hopeful that it would also fill Paul up. If he could hear me speaking God's Word, hopefully he would know that God had this all under control. And, hopefully this would keep his spirit a thankful one.

I was in such a better spirit that I left the hospital for a couple hours and went home to see the kids. I was able to be home to get Paulie off of the bus, and to spend some time with all three of our babies. I believe they saw the positive change in me. While they asked a few questions, they also seemed more able to handle the ambiguity of the situation. Even though I still didn't have any answers, I was able to share that their Daddy was a fighter. He was doing his very best to get better each day. And, God was definitely at work on healing their Daddy. That said, he still needed them to keep praying, and they all agreed. And then, we spent some good Mommy "snuggle time". I think they knew I needed that, too!

I also felt like God was working through my friends, as many started posting fun pictures from college for "Throwback Thursday" #tbt. I found myself checking Facebook more often that day, as God had provided additional support through the love of so many friends. I don't have words to describe how much I needed that or how perfect the timing was. I will be forever grateful!

When I arrived back at the hospital, I spent a few hours with Paul and then added my afternoon update during the evening shift change:

Thursday, February 26th, 8:12pm:
UPDATE: Well, today was an interesting day. They are trying to reduce Paul's sedation to determine when they can try to get him off the vent. The challenge is, when he wakes up - he thrashes. He is a very strong man and he uses all of his might. It is scary to watch!

Kidneys - he did make a little pee - Praise God! They are starting to pull 100 mL/hr. Please keep praying for healing his kidneys!

Lungs - because of the mix of meds, he has gone up and down on the vent all day. They tell me this is common - just hard to see. Based on this, it doesn't look like he will get the vent out tomorrow. Just praying for someday soon. And, when they do it, that his lungs will handle it on their own

Thank you all for your prayers! They really are working. And, thank you for the fun pictures today! They really did make me smile.

And then, when I got back into Paul's room after shift-change, I felt called to add this update to ask for specific prayers:

Thursday, February 26th, 10:00pm:
UPDATE: Paul's afternoon carried into the evening. After shift change, he was thrashing again. He needed multiple people to hold him down. When that happens, it starts a cycle:
- bolus of pain / sleep meds
- those meds drop BP
- lower BP makes it hard to pull more fluid through dialysis
- fluid on lungs makes it difficult to remove vent
- vent is main reason for his agitation.

I cannot imagine what he is going through. I have seen his eyes open. While they are still his amazing eyes, they are glassy and he looks very far away. They tell us he is in a sort of "groundhog's day". Due to all the sedation, he does not remember anything. Each time he wakes up, it's like it's the first time.

> Tonight's prayer requests:
> - pray for a good night sleep for everyone.
> - pray for the right mix of medicines to keep him calm, help him heal, and help him get off of the vent
> - pray for his kidneys.
>
> I will get the labs and send in morning report.
>
> Thank you for your prayers! God is performing miracles each day in Paul! And, we just know He will bring Paul fully back to us - in His time.

This was a true answer to prayer. I was able to be in there to see his eyes open. Even though they were glassy and he looked so far away, I was able to see his eyes. He was in there, and he was coming back to us...back to me. *Thank you, God, for allowing me to see that. You knew exactly what I needed!*

I was also so very happy that the nurses felt like it was okay for us to start talking to Paul again. We were able to hold his hand, and talk to him. They just asked us to talk quietly and try to stay away from his face. They were trying to keep him as calm as possible. That said, this allowed me to talk to him when he opened his eyes. I was able to tell him where he was and what the tube was. I would ask him not to bite down on the tube as it was helping him breathe. I told him I loved him, and I needed him to rest to let the medicine work. He was getting better, and I would be right by his side.

He would soon fall back asleep...or be given a bolus dose of sedation or pain meds because he was feisty, and when he woke up I would repeat the very same things. It was calming for me to say this to him. Even though I was repeating the same thing, it was both for his and my benefit. It was helping me to see all the progress.

As I prepared to get some rest that evening, I had a renewed sense of hope. When I rolled over on my couch to get a couple hours of rest, I thanked God for reopening my eyes to all the miracles He had already provided. While we still had a long road ahead of us, I felt His "peace beyond understanding." I knew He had this completely under control. He had already provided so much in the healing of Paul – and He wasn't finished yet. I just knew it. He was going to heal Paul. Paul was going to walk out of this hospital with me, hand-in-hand, going home to our kids.

Chapter 13: Filling My Soul and Praying for Paul's

Friday, February 27, 2015

That night was one of the most restful sleeps I had in the hospital. The overnight nurse was one who had been with Paul in the past, so we knew she had it under control. Beyond that, I just felt like God was showing us that He had this under control. Paul was in great hands (Heavenly Hands) and I needed my sleep. With that, I think I slept for a good six hours straight!

When my phone alarm went off at 6:00am, it was the first morning I remember waking up without the fear about what had happened during my rest. I walked into Paul's room and checked in with the nurse on what happened overnight. Here was the morning report:

> **Friday, February 27th, 7:26am:**
>
> UPDATE: Paul is a feisty man! He decided he no longer needed his OG tube (the tube pulling the acid out of his stomach), so he pulled it out. Thank God it wasn't the vent!
>
> Kidneys-his creatinine is down to 4.16! They were able to pull 100mL/hr all night! Keep praying for those kidneys!
>
> Lungs - he is still on 40 oxygen / 8 PEEP. They didn't try to move it last night. The good news is he has a 100% saturation rate!
>
> Meds - we are praying they can find the right balance of meds to keep him calm and awake (semi-awake). This will help them to ensure he is ready to get that vent out. Please pray for that!

> My additional prayer is for his spirit. While we have been seeing his improvement and Praising God for the miracles He is providing, Paul doesn't see that. When he wakes up, we cannot know what he will think about all of this - how he will feel. Please pray that he will see all of God's miracles through this journey. While it will not be easy or fast, God is moving the mountain one stone at a time. Praying for peace & patience for Paul.

Yes. The night when I finally gave in and got great rest, Paul decided to start pulling tubes. I was truly grateful it wasn't the vent. The doctors and nurses decided that it was okay to leave the OG tube out for a while. Depending on how Paul progressed the next day or so, they would decide if they needed to replace it.

Other than that, the updates were really positive. His kidneys seemed to be holding steady when on slow, continuous dialysis. His numbers continued to remain stable, and they were able to continue to pull fluid off of his body. He was still quite puffy – well, that's an understatement. When they stopped pushing fluids to keep Paul's blood pressure up, they had added ~20 liters of fluid...that's 44 lbs.! On the slow, continuous dialysis, the goal was to pull just over 1lb per day. At that rate, it would take us nearly six weeks to get all of the extra fluid removed. And, that was only if the dialysis machine ran continuously – meaning that it wouldn't clot or shut down for several hours. We were just so very thankful when the machine was working and they were able to pull the excess fluid. While we had a way to go, we were moving in the right direction.

We were also so very thankful to see that Paul was requiring less oxygen support. While he wasn't ready to get off of the vent, we were thankful we didn't wake up to a "setback" with his lungs. He was stable. And, for us at that time, stable was good.

We also asked for specific prayers for the pharmacists to find the best balance of pain and sedation medicines. While I knew this was what the pharmacists did best, I just felt like Paul was a special case (he probably wasn't). I was truly thankful for all they had done to keep Paul alive with the ability to recover. I prayed that would continue, and they would be able to keep him semi-awake and restful. I felt like I was asking for another mountain to be moved. That said, I felt called to make the request.

My last prayer request was for Paul's spirit. While my sister and I had prayed for this on Tuesday, I felt it was time to ask for more prayer support. I'm not sure how the community of prayer warriors felt about this request. Paul was still deep in the woods. He needed lots of physical healing. He was still "resting comfortably" – or, at times, not so comfortably. Maybe they felt my focus should be on his physical healing first and spirit second. But, I just felt like we were close. We were so close to witnessing the miracle of God's healing that I needed to ask for those prayers. I felt like it was time to get more people focused on his spirit. His body was showing signs of healing; we had no way of knowing what was happening with his spirit.

We had been blessed with many visitors throughout this week, and the weekend crowd had started to arrive. The hospital staff seemed to be taken aback by the volume of people who came to visit (not to mention the cards, flowers, care-packages, etc.). They had other patients that may get one or two visitors per day. Paul had a consistent three to five people at the hospital at all times. When they saw the additional visitors already starting to show up early Friday, they were truly stunned. We tried to share with them how amazing Paul is, and how many people we had praying for his healing. We couldn't wait for Paul to wake up so they could meet the person we were all praying for. For this incredible man (husband, father, son, brother, uncle, nephew, friend) to show the staff why an entire community lifted him up in prayer.

ICU Photo #2

That afternoon, while I was out of the room, another photo was taken of Paul. As with the other photo, I struggled with the decision to include it. However, since God ensured we had the photo, we felt He made the decision for us. This was what Paul looked like on Friday afternoon:

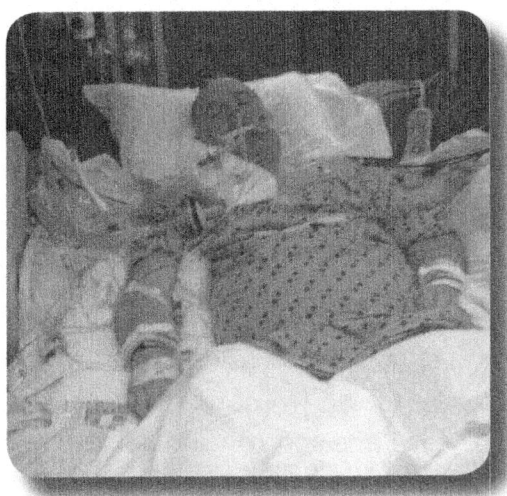

Friday, February 27th, ~2:00pm – This photo is more of a close-up. You can still see how puffy Paul is, even with the extra fluid being pulled off by dialysis. While you can still see all of the tubes, I see his color coming back. I can see his handsome face. I can see my Paul coming back to me.

Later in the afternoon, I had the opportunity to add this update on Paul's progress:

Friday, February 27th, 3:36pm:
UPDATE: I thought I would send a mid-day note today. Paul is resting comfortably-Hallelujah!!

Meds - some might be wondering why they keep changing his meds. This is important because they want him to be able to help when they want to take him off of the vent. Some meds are able to be onboard during those tests and some really should be off. So, they are trying to find the right mix to keep him just right. I think they have found it...for now.

Lungs - down to the lowest help - 30 oxygen / 5 PEEP. His oxygen level is still at 99-100 and has been all day - Praise God!!!

Kidneys - the doctor came in so I asked him about the creatinine. He said that the machine is what has dropped Paul's creatinine. So, while I was hoping that drop meant the kidneys were waking up, it just means the dialysis is doing its job. When Paul starts peeing more, that means they are starting to work again. And, he has had some output today. Not much, but some is better than none!

Me - so many of you have asked how I am doing. I haven't posted about it because I'm not really sure how to answer. I am trying to eat 3 meals a day and get 4-6 hours of sleep. Some days, I can be strong and deal with it all and others I feel broken and alone. While there are people here with me, my person is Paul. He is my rock, he is my love, he is my life.

For I can do everything through Christ, who gives me strength. (Philippians 4:13 NLT). And it is by God's strength and the strength everyone else is providing that is keeping me & the rest of the family going. Thank you so very much!

There was so very much in this update:

- Specific answer to a specific prayer – they had his meds worked out and he was resting comfortably.
- While some may have missed it, they were working on the medicine mix to help him get off of the vent. That meant they thought, sometime soon, he would no longer require the vent. Another answer to prayer!

- Reality – While we were thankful for the creatinine numbers coming down, I learned that it was just a reflection of the machine doing its job. We still needed specific prayers for Paul's kidneys, as our new measure of improvement would be urine output.
- My emotional state. This was hard to add into this post. So many had been doing the best they could to keep it together themselves, and to try to help me. I didn't want anyone to feel as though their efforts, their support, their prayers went unnoticed or unappreciated. That said, I often felt very alone. I would be in a roomful of people and feel alone. I am absolutely certain I pushed people away. I made others feel that I had it all together. When people asked what they could do, I told them I didn't need anything.

As I reflect back now, I couldn't focus on my emotional state. There were too many things that needed to be done. I needed to focus on Paul, our kids, our finances, etc. As for me, I needed to focus on my physical needs – food and sleep. My only other need was for Paul to wake up. I needed my partner. I needed my other half. I didn't feel whole without him. So, instead of people praying for me, I wanted everyone praying for him. Their prayers for him were for me, too. Having him wake up would make me whole. The rest would need to wait for another time – after Paul woke up.

I spent the rest of the day either in Paul's room, or talking with our many visitors – preparing them to see Paul. I cannot imagine what had filled their minds, so I wanted to help keep their focus on the positive – on the healing God had already provided. Regardless of what I said, the statistics and the visual were more than most could handle. He had been in the ICU, sedated and on life-support for nine days. While there were signs of improvement, he still looked very sick lying in that bed. And, there were no guarantees he was waking up.

While we had many visitors that week, there was one visitor I was especially thankful for. As you might remember, I had a friend who went through a similar experience a couple of years before. She helped me with the conversation with the kids, and had continually stayed in touch – providing me with great wisdom, guidance and prayers.

Early Friday morning, she sent a text that she would be available to visit. She could come that afternoon or later in the weekend, whatever worked best. I had such a mix of emotions. While I wanted to see her, I knew this would bring back a flood of memories about her experience. So, I tried to send the best message I could to help her hear my heart – I would love for her to come up, but I completely understood if it was too much.

Just after I finished the mid-afternoon update, there she was, in the ICU waiting room, and I fell into her arms. While I tried to keep it together for everyone else, she was the *only* person who had been here before. I couldn't hide it from her. And, I could see in her eyes that this was more of an emotional experience than she had anticipated, too. We spent some time in the waiting room connecting. I caught her up on Paul's progress that wasn't in the posts or in my text messages. She reflected on the time she was there with her husband seeing and hearing similar news.

After some time, I wanted to get back into Paul's room. However, I didn't want to leave her, and I couldn't ask her to come into his room. I think she could sense my internal conflict, as she asked if she could come with me to see Paul. I think I double-checked and triple-checked that she was truly ready to see Paul. He was still very sick. I knew this would bring up so many memories, so very many difficult memories. As you can probably imagine, she confirmed she wanted to join me, as she knew I was ready to be back in his room.

As we walked into Paul's room, we held each other close as the moment was filled with emotion. I don't think either of us were prepared for that experience. It was a lot for her to see – both to see Paul so very sick lying there and the memory of her husband in a very similar state. She reflected on her experience as the wife of the man lying in the hospital bed. She remembered how tough that was and she expressed how sorry she was that I had to go through it.

I knew exactly what she was saying. This was something that you never wanted anyone to have to go through – *no one!* And, while our experiences were different, they were also too similar. One day, we had a healthy husband ready to take on the world. The next, he was lying in a hospital bed on life-support, fighting for his life. There was nothing that could prepare you for that. And, when you're there, you pray no one else you know and love would ever have an experience similar to it.

But, there we were. Paul was fighting for his life and she was there to give me support. And, she was able to give me support in a way that no one else could because no one else I knew had ever been through such an experience. I cannot imagine how hard that time was for her. What she gave to me – through the discussion on how to talk with our kids, the texts and notes during the week, and visiting us in the hospital – was immeasurable! While I pray no one I know ever has to go through anything similar to this, I know that she was a perfect role model of the friend I hope to be to anyone in a similar situation. There are no words that can ever express my deep-hearted gratitude. No words…just eternal gratefulness!

And, God knew exactly what I needed. Having her there for me, to help me through the journey of the caregiver, gave me more strength than I realized. He ensured that we would be together to help strengthen me for what was yet to come. We still had a long road ahead, and I needed to be ready. We all did.

The rest of the day was again filled with welcoming in family and friends, and sharing Paul's journey. He had made additional progress during the day which was great news to report to all those who saw him. While he still looked very sick, he was definitely getting much better.

Here was the evening report on Paul's progress during the day:

> **Friday, February 27th, 10:30pm:**
>
> UPDATE: Paul had a pretty good day overall.
>
> Meds - they were able to get a good mix of meds today. He stirs some, but when we are in there, we can tell him "that tube is a vent. It's helping you breathe. Just a little longer. It will be out soon." And, since he is on versed, he does not remember it when he stirs again a few minutes later. Which, I am fine with because he opens those amazing eyes! I get to see my Paul in there and he is coming back to us!! Praising God for His amazing miracles!
>
> Lungs - he is on the lowest support - 30 Oxygen / 5 PEEP!! We will see what they think over the weekend. Not putting any dates anymore. Just praying for God's Perfect Timing on this.
>
> Kidneys-he made a little pee. We are thankful for that. Please keep praying for those kidneys.
>
> Thank you to everyone near & far. Please know we feel your love, support & prayers. Many blessings to you all!

It had truly been a great day of progress! The medicine balance seemed to be right, and his lung function was definitely moving in the right direction. He was at the level needed to pull him off the vent. That said, they needed him to listen and complete the breathing challenge before they would pull the vent. Considering he was still waking up quite feisty, they weren't sure when he would be ready to complete the challenge. While we were praying for that to happen soon, I didn't want to put a date on it. I didn't want anyone disappointed with his progress. He was continuing to improve. He was on the lowest breathing support there was on a ventilator. There was no room for disappointment – only for positive thinking and prayers.

As I settled on my ICU couch for the evening, I spent time in prayer, reading and reflecting on how many miracles God had already provided. On day one and two, we didn't think Paul would make it minutes, much less make it days. We were now closing day nine, and Paul was both alive and showing significant signs of improvement. Again, still a long road ahead – but at least we had a road! So many blessings. So many reasons to be thankful. And, still so many prayers.

"God, You have already provided so many miracles in bringing Paul to this point. That said, You (and only You) truly know the work that still needs to be done. Lord, I pray for Paul's complete healing. While I don't quite know what I need to ask for, You do. You know. And, only You can make this happen. Please, Lord! He has come so far. Please heal him. Please let him walk out of this hospital with me, hand-in-hand, going home to take care of our babies. Please!"

Chapter 14: Praise the Lord! Paul is Awake!

Saturday, February 28, 2015

When I woke up on Saturday morning, I was not expecting much change. People had told me that the weekend shift was not likely to make any significant changes, as they hadn't been with him all week and wouldn't likely be with him the next week. The goal was to keep him stable, with some small improvements. Our experience could not have been any more opposite of that expectation.

Paul Was Awake!

His eyes were open and he was responding to commands. He could blink his eyes, squeeze his hands, and move his feet. When I told him *"I love you"*, he would respond with the sign language sign for "I love you". He was there. He was back. *What an answer to prayer!*

Then, during morning rounds, the pulmonologist was reviewing Paul's progress and felt it was time to have him complete the breathing challenge. This was when they would turn down both the oxygen support and the PEEP and have Paul breathe on his own for an hour. This was even more difficult than you could imagine because the vent tube was still down his throat. While it wasn't easy, Paul passed with flying colors.

One quick note – I told Paul that the test was an hour, and then they would take out the vent. What I didn't know was that, for some patients, even passing the test does not mean the vent would be removed right away. One nurse told me she had a patient who did this three times before the vent was removed. I felt terrible as I had gotten everyone's hopes up that the vent would be removed soon – especially Paul's.

I stopped right then and prayed that God would allow the vent to be removed, and that Paul would continue to improve without needing it.

The respiratory therapist turned the vent back on to 30% / 5 PEEP and we all waited for the doctors. Here was my post:

> **Saturday, February 28th, 11:20am:**
> Praising our Glorious God for such a great night / morning!
>
> Lungs: they had Paul try a breathing challenge - turned vent off - and he passed with flying colors!!! They are rounding soon and we will see when we can get that out - maybe today, maybe tomorrow. Keep praying! It's working!
>
> Kidneys: he peed!! Just a little bit. 50mL, but he peed!! His creatinine is down to 4. Keep praying for pee!
>
> Paul: he is more awake. Still not fully aware. He does remember some things between naps. He gave me the "i love you" sign with his hands. We are trying to help him talk / write. He's still on too many meds to allow that to work.
>
> Platelets: are up to 140!!! 150 is lower limit of normal so we are almost there!!!
>
> Will post more later. Please keep praying!! We have a Magnificent God who is working miracles!! Amen!

Truly, what a glorious morning! I went to bed thinking I would be thankful for stable, and woke up to Paul being awake and successfully completing a breathing challenge. Our next step was to wait for the doctors to round to determine when the vent could come out. Each minute seemed like an hour because I promised Paul, if he passed, that tube would come out. I knew not to promise what I couldn't deliver on, but I thought I was right. Unfortunately, I wasn't. It was up to the doctors, and we needed to be patient. They had other sick patients to see. And, Paul was no longer the *"sickest person in the hospital"* so they no longer visited his room first. Just as others had done for us, we needed to be patient and allow the doctors to see the sicker patients. It was a mixed blessing.

Just before 1:00pm, the doctors rounded on Paul and the pulmonologist agreed that it was time to pull the vent. *Praise God! Hallelujah!* While he needed to keep it on for an extra hour or so, at least it wasn't a few extra days. The doctor felt it was time to let Paul breathe on his own. He felt his lungs could handle it.

With that news, I added this post:

- **Saturday, February 28th, 12:59pm:**
  VENT IS COMING OUT!!!! PRAISE GOD!!!

What was amazing was that Paul was up that entire time. He was up for the breathing challenge, he was up while waiting for rounds, and he was up just before they removed the ventilator. He was awake!

When the vent was removed, they increased Paul's sedation so he could tolerate the procedure. When he woke up, they asked him to limit how much he spoke and to talk quietly for the first few hours. That was really tough for Paul. He had so many questions. That said, the sedation medicines were still flowing through his system. So, he didn't remember the answers. Not only that, he didn't remember who had been in the room just moments before. Let me share with you an experience we had.

Paul was pretty much asleep during the removal of the vent. When he woke up, his parents were in the room with him. He had a lot of questions, but his first ones were – *"What happened? Why am I here? Was I in a car accident? Was Jenn with me? Is she hurt? Where is my wife?"*

I had just been in his room less than thirty minutes prior. He was giving me the *"I love you"* sign and trying to communicate with me as much as he could. When he woke up again, he didn't know that I was alive or if anything happened. I wasn't expecting that to happened.

His sister had walked into the room, and his parents sent her to get me. As you can imagine, upon hearing this news, I raced into his room. I wanted to hold his hand and hear his voice. I needed him so very much, and it broke my heart that he didn't know that I was there. What made it even worse was that he didn't remember what brought him there. He thought we had been in a car accident and he worried that I was hurt in the process. I was so very thankful I could run into his room moments later to put that concern to rest. I wasn't hurt. I was fine. I was right there. And, I wouldn't leave him.

We weren't expecting Paul to wake up, so we also weren't expecting the number of visitors Paul would have walking through his room that day. We were just so very happy he was awake. And, since we had so many people praying, we wanted them to be able to see the miracle with their own eyes. Paul was awake – and they had a part in that. We didn't want to turn anyone away.

We obviously started with family. Paul spent time with all of us individually or in groups of two or three. He seemed to be pretty alert and aware of his surroundings. He knew each of us (Praise God! While we didn't think he would have any mental deficit, it was amazing that he woke up and knew everyone). He asked some questions and seemed to remember most of the answers. He really seemed like he was back. While his physical strength and kidneys still needed work, mentally, he appeared to be 100% with us.

With that in mind, I knew the kids had been patiently waiting to talk with their Daddy. They had no idea about the magnitude of his illness; they only knew they needed to keep praying. Now that Paul was awake, I hoped he could at least call the kids to say hello and let them hear his voice. I knew it would be a lot for Paul to handle, but I also knew all three of them would truly benefit from hearing their Daddy's voice. Paul agreed, so we made a quick call home. It definitely wasn't time for a video call yet. The voice call would have to be enough.

Paul talked with the kids for a couple of minutes. While the call wasn't long, you could hear the hope and joy in our children's voices! They had been praying for their Daddy to get better, and they were able to now know that their Daddy was at least able to talk with them. Of course, they wanted to know when Daddy was going to come home, to which we truly didn't have an answer. We said it would still be some time, but Daddy was getting better and their prayers helped in that. We asked them to keep praying and let them know how much we both loved each of them. They sent their love back and we ended the call.

It was an emotional call for Paul. While he agreed to it, I don't think either of us realized just how tough it would be. Paul still didn't fully grasp all that had happened to him, or how sick he was. He had learned that he had been in the hospital for ten days, under sedation the entire time. So, while he knew he wanted to assure the kids that he was awake, he didn't expect how difficult it would be to hear their voices – to hear the concern in their voices and their joy of talking with their Daddy. He and I spent some time together, reflecting on what had happened, and how thankful we both were for all God had provided. Again, Paul still had a lot of healing to do, but we needed to be thankful for all God had already provided – not many expected him to live, let alone wake up and be talking with the family. This was a miracle, and we needed to pause and share our thankfulness.

After a little while, we both seemed to have gotten it back together. I let Paul know that there were family and friends in the waiting room who were hoping to see him. He agreed, so we started to have people come back to see him. They did not expect him to be awake, so what a wonderful surprise and blessing it was to talk with Paul. And, Paul did his best to connect with each person.

As the day progressed, I noticed Paul wasn't fully himself. While he was awake, his mind wasn't as clear as we thought it was. He started saying things that didn't make complete sense. He also started to mix people up. And, he was asking questions about things that didn't happen. For example, he thought we had been on a helicopter going to an event in Las Vegas at the MGM Grand. He had such a vivid image of this experience; he could not believe that it didn't happen. Not wanting to frustrate him, I went along with the story and asked additional questions. I encouraged those who came into his room to not discount his visions. There would be time to differentiate truth from visions. At that moment, I just wanted him alive, awake and calm. They agreed.

While I didn't spend much time out of Paul's room, I was able to slip out for a moment and add this post:

> **Saturday, February 28th, 5:09pm:**
> UPDATE: I couldn't wait until evening. Paul is back! I mean really back! He is still letting the meds wear off, but he is with us!
>
> I can send reports on numbers tomorrow. For tonight, we are Praising God!
>
> As you can imagine, today was a big day for Paul. He woke up and had lots of people with him. He also knows he has been under for 10 days. That has rocked him quite a bit - as you could only imagine.
>
> He did quickly talk to the kids. He was sad, but said hi and he loves them! Hallelujah!! God is Amazing!!!
>
> He also has his sense of humor on full charge. He is cracking jokes (which also helps him not break down).

> I will post more when I know. Until then - Thank You! You have all helped us through this journey. Whether near or far, your prayers, posts, messages, support means more than we can ever describe. We love you all!
>
> To God goes the Glory! Amen!

As I returned to Paul's room, I could tell that he seemed even more confused than before. He was talking more about the visions and truly wasn't acting like himself. Just before shift change, I was talking with a nurse about some of what Paul was saying. She confirmed it was normal, and suggested we should limit his visitors for a while. He had just been through so very much, and needed time to rest.

Having been in the pharmaceutical field for over sixteen years, I had heard the term "ICU Psychosis", but I never truly understood what that meant...until now. While we were so very thankful that Paul was awake and we wanted everyone to see him, I started to see that he truly wasn't ready. There would be more time for people to visit with him. *Hallelujah! There would be more time.* But, at the moment, we needed him to rest. That meant, asking visitors to please understand – if they wanted to visit us in the waiting room – that was great. As for Paul, he needed time to rest, so seeing him would have to wait.

I shared my concern and request with the family that evening. I don't think they truly got the reasons for my request. They wanted to wait until morning to see how he was doing. There were lots of additional family members coming down to see Paul awake. They thought Paul would be able to handle it. While I doubted the night would make a difference, I agreed to wait until morning.

Late that evening, I was talking with Paul about the rules. No one was allowed to sleep in the ICU room. So, I told him I would stay up as long as possible, but when I got sleepy, I would need to go back to the waiting room. I would have someone else there with him, so he wasn't alone. That said, I would need to leave at some point.

Paul wouldn't have it. He was showing signs of significant paranoia and didn't want me to leave. He was seeing specific visions and was very scared. He thought that, if I left, he would not be alive. These visions were not just visions to him. They were real people, real things. And, if I left, he feared for both of our lives.

I spoke with the nurses, and they agreed to allow me to stay with him that evening. When he fell asleep, I would be able to leave and get some rest. Until then, I was allowed to stay in his room. So, I asked the rest of the family to get some sleep. While I was hoping I would stay up and Paul would sleep, there was the chance that I would need reinforcement during the evening. And, I wanted whoever it was stepping in to be fresh for Paul. It looked like he was going to need it.

Chapter 15: Awake ≠ Aware

Sunday, March 1, 2015

As the night progressed, Paul seemed to get worse. His eyes would dart around the room as if he was trying to find a flying object that would never stand still. During the day, he would only share a small bit about his visions. That night, he started sharing more:

- He saw a man in the back of the room smoking marijuana. He knew there was a no smoking rule, so Paul was worried that guy would get him kicked out of the hospital. That said, Paul didn't want to anger the man because he was very scary.
- Hanging from the ceiling was a metal chain that had several links where the IV bags could be hung. Paul thought those were the "devil's chains". He was fearful of being strung up by those chains and hung.
- As I was standing with my back to the wall and window (without any artwork), Paul told me how much he liked my artwork. He then shared that he *"didn't like the ones with the blood very much"*, but the others were nice.
- There was a light at the bottom of the television that would shine when it was on. At the top and bottom of the screen, there was a black line. Paul thought that he had to keep his eyes open and keep the light on the television above the black line. If the light would fall below, he would die.

He had other visions that he shared; those – along with the helicopter ride to the MGM Grand for a launch party – were the most detailed visions. To say this was a scary evening would be an understatement. We prayed together, and sang Christian songs. While it would calm him for a while, it did not take the fear away. And, every time I would drift off to sleep, he would wake me up. He was angry when I would fall asleep because he felt I was giving in and I was willing to die. We both needed to stay awake. To him, it was truly life or death.

> **Note:** *Some may wonder why I chose to add this information to the book. I could have left it out. Why share the details now?*
>
> *The reason is, that if you ever have a loved one in the ICU under sedation for several days, this is a possible scenario you might experience. Even knowing this was possible, I had never heard or understood just how scary this could be – both for the patient and the caregiver. So, while I know this is personal and hard, I truly want to help you understand our experience – to help you gain a perspective, in case you ever need it. And, I pray you never need it!*

As the sun came up, Paul and I hadn't gotten much, if any sleep. We may have drifted for a minute or two, but not much. Just before shift change, the nurse could see that we didn't get any sleep. She recommended that we limit visitors for Paul that day. He needed some time to rest and heal. And, while she thought my being there with him might help, it didn't look like either of us were in great shape. She had requested we not come back in right after shift change. She wanted to give Paul some time to try to relax on his own. If he needed me, she would get me. She needed me to get a couple hours of sleep and wanted to see how Paul would do alone.

While I didn't want to leave Paul, I also knew she was right. Not knowing what that night was going to bring, I would need to catch up on as much sleep as possible. He needed me, and I needed to be ready. I shared this information with our family, sent this update, and tried to get some sleep.

> **Sunday, March 1st, 8:58am:**
>
> UPDATE: Paul had a rough night last night. As you can only imagine, he received a lot of information yesterday. And, while we tried to keep it at a high level, it was still a lot to take in.
>
> And, because we didn't know he would be waking up, he had a lot of visitors yesterday (I just counted 17 and I may have missed a few) which was so very emotional for both sides - Paul and the visitors.
>
> The nurses have asked to give him a few hours of no visitors, and to limit visitors today to only a few to allow him time to rest.
>
> Please know - God gave Paul back to us. We will have him for a long time. I know we all want to see him and hold him and love on him - me included. However, we need to do what's best for him right now.
>
> Please know that everyone is welcome to come to the hospital. We are in the waiting room and truly appreciate the company. Please also know that might mean not seeing Paul. At least not today. We will see what tomorrow brings.
>
> Thank you for understanding!

As I rested on the ICU couch trying to fall asleep, I was hoping I did the right thing. I didn't want to turn anyone away. So many people had been praying for Paul; they were part of helping to bring about this miracle. How could I ask them to stay away? How could I ask them not to visit and not to see, with their own eyes, the miracle God had provided? As I drifted off to sleep, I felt conflicted. I prayed for an answer. I prayed for peace. I prayed for Paul to continue to heal and for the community to continue to pray. He definitely needed them!

As I got a little sleep, Paul was in his room alone. The nurses were hoping this would be helpful – allowing him to calm himself and not rely on me to help him. While this works for many patients, it was not working for Paul. He definitely needed someone in there with him – and he wanted that person to be me. He worried that something would happen to both of us whenever we were apart. He begged the nurse to please bring me back into the room. She could see that he was getting increasingly agitated, so she agreed.

When the nurse came out to get me, she saw I was sleeping. She asked Paul's parents to come in to be with him to try to give me a little more time to sleep. None of us could understand what the day would hold, and I needed to be prepared.

About 10:00am, I woke up and looked at my phone. Paul had asked his mom for her phone and was sending me text messages. He missed me. He wanted me in the room with him. He didn't want to be apart from me. It broke my heart that he was missing me. I didn't want him to be sad. I felt selfish for sleeping. Even though I knew my body needed it, I felt like he needed me more. I was so disappointed in myself.

I ran back into Paul's room. When he saw me, he was even more agitated and worried than I anticipated from reading his texts. Even with his parents there, he was worried something happened to me. He didn't know why I wasn't with him. He needed me there – always.

Chapter 16: No Time for Sleep

Sunday, March 1, 2015

Just before noon, the nurse came in to share that she wanted to get Paul up and into a chair. She shared the process of doing this – Paul would not need to exert much effort. They would pull a fabric sling underneath him and hook it up to a machine that would lift him up and move him over. They would settle him into the chair, where they were hoping he would sit for at least an hour.

While we were nervous, it was also exciting hearing about progress. They wanted to get him up and requiring some movement. That was great news! I didn't know what to expect from Paul, but was looking forward to seeing his strength baseline. It was just a starting point.

Before they were able to move Paul, the dialysis machine started whirring and alarming. If you have never heard a dialysis machine alarm, it is something else! So, the nurses came in and realized the machine had clotted off again. They had to unhook Paul and talk with the nephrologists about next options. Now that Paul was awake, one option would be regular hemodialysis (the one that cycles your blood much faster and can pull off more fluid in each session).

So, minor setback, but we were ready to get Paul in the chair. He and I looked through the movies on demand and chose *Finding Nemo*. We would have a little "date night" (well really "date afternoon") watching a movie and holding hands.

As they put the fabric tarp under Paul, I could already see how weak he had become. He could barely help them move him. He couldn't really roll over. He could barely touch his mouth with his hand. His legs were like Jell-O. He definitely had lost his strength. That said, they were able to lift him and get him into a chair. As I looked at him, he looked so weak. Just two weeks prior, he was playing full court basketball with his friends. He was strong and healthy. Now, he didn't even have the strength to keep his head up. His head was continually flopped over to the right. When I asked him to see if he could straighten his neck, he was barely able to move it. He definitely had quite a lot of work to do to regain his strength. It was then he asked with tear-filled eyes,

"Will I ever be able to walk again? Will I be able to take care of the kids? Will I get back to playing basketball or will I be like this?"

While I didn't have an answer for him, I had seen what God had already done to heal Paul. He and I prayed that God would help Paul regain his strength and provide complete healing. I also committed to asking the next doctor who visited us.

Before our "date hour" was up, Paul was feeling pretty tired. While he wanted to have the nurse put him back into bed, he didn't want me to go ask her – even though the nurses' station was just outside the room. Even those few seconds were more than he wanted to handle. That said, I knew I needed to give him small moments alone if he was going to get through this mentally. So, I told him I would be right back, and went out to find the nurse and ask her to put Paul back into his bed. And, she did.

The hope was that this movement – getting him up, out of bed, sitting in a chair – would make Paul sleepy. He woke up on Saturday morning and had basically been awake since then. Unfortunately, Paul didn't fall asleep right away, but they were able to calm him enough to help him sleep a little that evening. The nurses also allowed me to stay in his room again, just until he fell asleep. Then, I would be able to go back to the couch.

Paul fought it for a while, but just after 11:00 pm, he (or his body) finally gave in and he fell asleep. While I wanted to stay with him, I was completely exhausted. I walked into the ICU waiting room, curled up on the couch and added this post:

Sunday, March 1st, 11:34pm:
UPDATE: Paul is finally resting today. I think he went 36 hours with very little sleep. Thank you all for understanding his need for sleep & quiet today. Praying each day gets better so he can see everyone!! This has just been very overwhelming for Paul as he didn't know why he was in the hospital. He thought we were in a car accident.

Kidneys - we had to turn off dialysis. Another clot :(. Good news is that he is stable enough for regular dialysis - likely to start tomorrow. So, while his creatinine is up, he is peeing more and more. That should help!

Lungs - he is breathing well without the vent! Still on nasal cannula and doing great!

Platelets - back into the normal range - HALLELUJAH!!

New News:
We will likely leave ICU tomorrow for a regular room. That will help him rest more. And, I will be able to stay with him - AMEN TO THAT!!!

Paul thanks everyone for your support & prayers. Praying for a restful sleep, for a peaceful mind, for his kidneys to kick in and for his muscles to get back to work.

Much love to everyone!!

It wasn't thirty minutes after I clicked send on the evening update that the nurse came to find me. He was awake again and asking for me. He was worried that something happened, so they were willing to let me stay with him in the room.

We didn't get much sleep that night. Paul was seeing just as many visions as he had the night before. Most were the same visions, although a couple new ones popped up. I sat next to his bed in a chair, holding his hand, trying to snuggle up as close as I could.

My problem was that my body was so tired. I had gotten very little sleep – really almost no sleep at all. As much as I tried, I couldn't keep my eyes open. The true blessing that night was that Paul was willing to try to close his eyes for a few minutes at a time. I started with asking for five minutes. I asked if we could try to close our eyes for just five minutes. I promised him everything would be okay. I was here. I wasn't leaving. That said, we both needed some sleep. He agreed to five minutes. I think it might have lasted two minutes.

This went on a few times during the night before I finally gave up asking. We spent the night talking about so many different topics. The one specific thing Paul asked was to have me turn on my music. What an answer to prayer!

> ***Note:*** *I know I have written about me turning on my music, I guess I should give more details. I have an iTunes library of over 150 contemporary Christian songs. I absolutely love Christian music, and I am so very thankful for Christian artists! When I shared before that the kids would see me tear up in the car from a song, it was almost always on K-LOVE, Air-1 or SiriusXM's The Message. At the back of this book, I have added some of my favorites. While my favorites change all the time, I have many that are always perfect.*

Remember when my sister and I were praying for Paul's spirit, and when I made the specific prayer request that Paul would wake up with a thankful heart? This was the first outward sign that he was seeking additional comfort from Christ. He wasn't mad, angry or bitter. He was thankful. He was a bit out of his mind with all of the sedation medicines still wearing off, but the aware side of him was asking for more, wanting to listen to the songs to feel closer to Jesus. Truly, Praise God! If the other miracles God provided weren't enough, this was 100% a specific answer to a specific prayer. There was no doubt about it, no other explanation. This was God!

We spent the rest of the night singing "my music". One song that seemed to really connect with Paul was Kari Jobe's song, *I am not alone*. We replayed that song a few times that night, and Paul would well up with tears. He was alive, he was awake, he was thankful, and he was seeking. That could only be God! *Thank You! Hallelujah and Amen!*

Chapter 17: Moving Day – When One Door Closes

Monday, March 2, 2015

It took quite a while for Paul to finally fall asleep. He may have gotten an hour of sleep prior to shift change at 7:00am. The nurse came in which meant it was time for me to leave. Since Paul was finally sleeping, I felt it was okay to go. Plus, he hadn't slept much in two days, so I was hopeful he would be asleep for some time. As I walked out of his room and into the waiting room, I added this update:

> **Monday, March 2nd, 6:56am:**
>
> UPDATE: Paul is finally resting! I am almost afraid to write that as I do not want to jinx it. He went nearly 48 hours with very little sleep - 10-15 minute naps here & there. I'm just so glad he is sleeping!
>
> I don't have any of the labs yet. I will add those to a later post. I would assume his creatinine is up as he has been off dialysis for 1.5 days. So, we will wait & see.
>
> Today's prayer requests:
> - Rest for Paul. He needs it!
> - Hemodialysis - praying that clears his body of the residual medicines (sedation/pain).
>
> And, happy birthday to Paul's mom, Patti. While I know this isn't how she expected to spend her birthday, seeing Paul wake up and all of his improvements have been an amazing gift!

What a true blessing! We were so hopeful that Paul would wake up sometime before his mom's birthday. We were hopeful it would happen, but we didn't want to put any dates on it, as we didn't want to make the day or the progress disappointing. But, here we were on his mom's birthday, and he was alive, awake, and talking! They would start the hemodialysis, which would allow them to clean the blood quicker and hopefully start pulling off more of the fluid. Again, he was still quite puffy. Plus, they were planning on moving us to a non-ICU room.

Before they would move Paul out of the ICU, they wanted to do one hemodialysis treatment in his room. They wanted to ensure he could tolerate the treatments before moving him to the non-ICU room. The reason – once in a non-ICU room, the patient goes to the dialysis unit. Considering that, it was important to know how Paul would tolerate the treatment before they sent him to the unit. As we were waiting for the dialysis technician to arrive, I was able to add this update:

Monday, March 2nd, 1:17pm:
UPDATE: Today has been a very busy day for Paul!

Lungs - he is still on nasal cannula and doing great!

Kidneys - waiting for dialysis. Creatinine spiked pretty high. He will have the dialysis today so numbers should drop. Key will be Wed morning numbers.

Physical strength - doctor said it will take ~3 days of exercises for every 1 day in the ICU. He had both PT & OT here today.

Food - Paul's feeding tube was removed, so he was able to have a Popsicle, some Jell-O, lemon ice & Sprite. Yummo!

All other labs look good or improving!

Sleep - he still needs to catch up on sleep. Hopefully, we will get up to the new room & both get some good sleep tonight.

Praying for kidneys to start working & sleep!

Will see if we have more news by end of day. Much love & thank you for praying!!

Two points:

First – I had very mixed emotions about moving rooms. The positives were that Paul no longer required the support of the ICU. He was improving, and he was no longer the "sickest person in the hospital." They believed he would make it, and now we just needed to focus on healing the damage the toxins did to his body, specifically to his kidneys. That said, I was also nervous and sad. The ICU nurses had taken such great care of Paul. They knew him, they knew our story, and they had been with us from the start of this journey. We had trusted them with everything, and they did everything they could to keep Paul alive and get him to this point. While the other nurses were likely good people, I knew the attention would be less. Yes, that was because Paul didn't require the constant attention. However, that was what we had become accustomed to, and I wasn't sure I was ready to let that go.

Second - Something I decided not to share in this post was the phone call with my team leader from work. As you may recall, we knew there were plans for realignments at work, and it was highly likely that my position would be eliminated. Mid-afternoon I received an e-mail asking if I was available to talk, so I called him right away. I had come to terms with any decision the organization made, and I didn't want to postpone the call. I truly wanted the discussion done so I could move on, take care of Paul, and not worry about the "potential" news. I would have the answers.

So, I called him right away and he answered. I could tell by the sound of his voice, my expectations were confirmed. My position was eliminated. Having been through these several times, both on the delivering and receiving end, I knew what was coming. Before he could share the necessary talking points, I let him know that I knew what was coming, I was at peace with the decision, and he didn't need to worry. I would listen to the information he needed to share, and we could talk in greater detail about it sometime later. My only question was – was I eligible for severance? While he said that was an option, he wanted me to know that there were other options to stay and I was a highly valued colleague. He didn't want me to jump to that being my only option. That said, even at that moment, I could feel God's plan coming to fruition. Even though I didn't know what would happen next, I felt God showing me that He had this all under control. He just saved Paul; He would see us through this. There wasn't any need to worry about this right now. It was time to focus on Paul. Time to focus on our family. The rest would all come in due time. While many Bible verses came to mind, these two were particularly helpful:

> ***Romans 8:31-32 (GNB):***
> *In view of all of this, what can we say? If God is for us, who can be against us? Certainly not God, who did not even keep back His Own Son, but offered Him for us all! He gave us His Son – will He not also freely give us all things?*
>
> ***Jeremiah 29:11 (GNB):***
> *I alone know the plans I have for you, plans to bring you prosperity and not disaster, plans to bring about the future you hope for.*

I didn't know what God's plan was for us, for me, but I knew that He had a plan, and I needed to be patient and obedient. He was setting the stage. There was no time to worry about that when there were more important things to worry about.

> *I engaged the community in prayer about this the next day, so you will see that post shortly. For now, let's get back to focusing on Paul...*

As you can imagine, Paul was so very thankful he was able to have something to eat. If you remember, he wanted water or ice chips in the ER twelve days before, but they wouldn't give him any. They were too afraid he would vomit. The EMS professionals saw that in the ambulance and wanted to ensure that didn't happen again! So, Paul had been twelve days without anything "real" to eat. He had nutrition flowing through his tubes, so he wasn't starving. That said, it was different getting the nutrition through a tube versus eating something of substance. Eating that food – well, clear liquid food – was over-the-moon exciting for him. He had waited so long, and he was so very appreciative. He took his time, savored every bite, and wanted more when it was all done. We had come so far, and we were so thankful.

Just past noon, the dialysis technician arrived to start the hemodialysis. Since Paul was able to tolerate the slow, continuous dialysis, we all hoped he would tolerate this, too. That said, it is quite different, so we were all cautiously optimistic for this new procedure. And, Paul did amazing! The technician was able to do a full 3.5-hour run, and she was able to pull off 4lbs of excess fluid. If you remember, with the slow, continuous dialysis, the goal was ~1lb per day. So, this new treatment would allow the technicians to pull significantly more fluid off of Paul. He was already looking less puffy, and we knew this new treatment would help speed that process.

We were also so very thankful that Paul tolerated the treatment, as it also removed some of the excess medicines in his system. Paul still wasn't making much urine, so as the medicines broke down in his body, there wasn't a way to get them out of his system. And, even the little urine Paul was making did not ensure any of the excess was being removed. We were hopeful that the hemodialysis would remove much of the excess medicine to help his mind. Well, I was extremely hopeful and prayerful that this treatment would help heal his mind. Those visions were so scary, and he was definitely not himself. We would be moving to the regular medical unit for the evening, so I would be able to sleep in his room with him on a real pull out bed. Hallelujah! But, I was worried that we would have another scary night of visions.

"Please God, let this treatment heal Paul's mind. He has been through so much, and You have provided so many miracles. I pray for one more tonight. Please heal his mind. Please let this work!"

Paul finished the dialysis around 5:00pm, and the nurses started the process to get Paul moved to the non-ICU medical unit. We were so thankful when we learned Paul would be moved to a unit on the same floor, just down the hall. The second floor had become our home for the previous twelve days. It was nice to not have to find another new home.

Packing up Paul's room was filled with more emotions than I was prepared for. Tears streamed down my face as I pulled the pictures off of the wall and packed up the gifts we had received. We had been so very blessed by everyone lifting Paul up in prayers. We could truly feel the love, support and prayers of the entire community. And, it worked! Paul had made it. He was alive, and now needed less support than before. While he was still sick, he was definitely not *the sickest person in the hospital*. There would be another patient needing this room, and it was time for us to start the next chapter in the journey.

We got our things together, moved into our new room down the hall, and got settled in for however long that next part would take. Here was my evening update on the day:

Monday, March 2ⁿᵈ, 9:17pm:
UPDATE: Paul had an exhausting day - all good, just a really big day. Here is the rundown:
- Catheter Removed
- Feeding Tube Removed
- Able to have "clear liquids" which included two popsicles
- Hemodialysis - 3.5 hours of a faster dialysis where they pulled off 4lbs of excess fluid
- Changed room - now out of ICU.

I am exhausted, and I didn't do any of the work.

The good news is that I have my own chair/bed in his room so I can be near him. Amen to that!

Still need prayers for kidneys, strength & clarity of mind.

Praise God for all of the positive activity today! What a way to start a new week!

It truly was a good day. It had its ups and downs. It was full of emotion. And, I would soon learn it wasn't over yet.

Chapter 18: Tomorrow is Never Guaranteed – A Commitment to Our Marriage

What's amazing about life, especially when you are young, is the belief that there will always be time. There will be time to say, "I love you". There will be time to make amends. There will always be time to explain what happened. There will be time.

But, what if there isn't time? What happens if you go from healthy one day to a life-threatening illness, causing you to be in a medically induced coma on life-support, the next? What if you don't wake up? What if you don't have time?

I share this with you because when Paul woke up, when his mind was clear and he had time to think about our lives before the infection, he realized there were a couple of things he needed to confess. So, after everyone else left his room for the evening, Paul opened up about two things he had been keeping from me.

Now, these were not marriage ending things, but they were things he had been hiding from me. While I will not give specifics out of respect for Paul, I will share that these do not include anything to do with adultery, substance abuse, pornography, etc. Again, they were not marriage ending things, but still difficult to hear. I thought we had full and complete trust in our marriage. There wasn't anything I didn't share with Paul, and I believed he did the same. So, learning that he lied to me, or that he hid something from me, just took my breath away. Here I was, so happy that he was alive and finally clear-minded, and now this.

That night was filled with a great deal of emotion. We would have to stop our conversation several times for the nurses to come in to do vitals, give medicines, etc. I'm sure they were wondering why we were both crying, but that wasn't any of their business. They just completed their task and left, and then we got back to our conversation. We weren't yelling at each other. We were speaking in normal tones and crying.

There were three things about this that were especially hard for me:

- First, that he did these things at all was disappointing. But, that he decided to then lie about them hurt even worse. That meant, he knew that what he was doing would upset me, yet he did it anyway. And, instead of being truthful when he did it and discussing it like a loving couple, he decided to hide it – to avoid the conversation.
- Coming to terms with believing those were the only things he was hiding. If he was willing and able to hide those things from me, what else was he hiding? I thought we had a completely transparent marriage. If he can hide some things, there must be more that he hasn't told me. If he was going to come clean, let's get it all out.
- What would have happened if he didn't wake up? Where would my mind have gone if I didn't have the chance to talk through this with him? What else would I have believed to be true? He wouldn't be able to tell me himself, and my mind would have been filled with a lot of misinformation.

I just sat there in a swirl of emotions. I was sad that he felt compelled to do these things and then lied about them. I was mad that he lied – to me, hiding the truth is the same as telling a lie. No difference. I was happy that he was awake and we were able to talk this through. I was concerned that there was more he wasn't telling me. I was trying to come up with what it was in our marriage that caused him to do this. And, I didn't want to ever be in this situation again. So, while I wasn't letting him "off the hook", no additional conversation about this would change the facts.

We committed to having an open and honest relationship from that day forward –

NO SECRETS, NO HALF-TRUTHS, NO HIDING ANYTHING.

What we were also able to do was to recommit to our marriage. The marriage we both wanted to have. We committed to an everyday reminder to love and respect each other, and not take each other for granted. We agreed that each morning, Paul would ask me to marry him, and each night, I would ask him to marry me. This would help us start and end our day focused on being the people we wanted to be. I want to be the woman Paul wants to be married to, the woman he deserves. I am so thankful that he also wants to be the man I want to be married to. So, while it wasn't easy, and there are still days when my mind drifts back to the *"what else"* thoughts, we were able to make it through and have found ways to help us never go back.

> **<u>Note:</u>** *Just like with the visions, you may wonder, why am I sharing this? This story could have definitely been shared without these details. And, you are absolutely right. That said, this was such an important part to where we are as a couple today. We are better together, we are better parents, and we are better friends today because of this. And, if Paul didn't wake up, it would have been a completely different story. I am so very thankful God provided the miracles to heal Paul and gave him the presence of mind to share those things with me. Had that not have happened, I would always have wondered what else I didn't know. Paul is such an amazing, loving, caring man. That is the man I am supposed to always remember.*

So, I am sharing this because we all believe that we will be here tomorrow. But, what if that is not true? Is there anything you are holding onto that, if you weren't here to explain, would hurt your loved ones? Is there anything that you are hiding that is driving a wedge in your relationship? If there is, you need to decide when the right time is to share that information. Maybe it's now, maybe it's not. Just remember, tomorrow is never guaranteed. And, if you aren't there to answer questions, those questions will be answered for you – in ways you cannot control, and likely with a lot of misinformation. It's not easy having those talks, and there is no guarantee that the outcome will be a better, more loving relationship. It's just something to think about...

One more thing – as I looked back at that night, I was focused on the fact that I hadn't lied to Paul. I had been fully honest with him and expected that he was fully honest with me. As I thought this through, I realized that I had ownership in this situation, too. While I was always honest with Paul, I wasn't always available.

As you have likely recognized, I had been dedicating a lot of time to work and volunteer "relationships" and didn't spend the same amount of time or dedication to the relationships that mattered the most – the ones with my husband and our children. So, I had ownership in this. I was also at fault. This wasn't one-sided. And, I needed to commit my time and focus to the relationships that mattered the most:

God, Paul and our kids

After a while, we were both exhausted – emotionally, mentally and physically. We had cried so much; I think our eyes were incapable of making any more tears. And, while it was a difficult conversation, we both knew just how blessed we were to be having the conversation. How different life would have been had God not saved Paul. We needed to be thankful and prayerful.

I looked into Paul's puffy, red eyes and asked, *"Will you marry me?"* He looked back at my tear-stained face and with a shaky voice replied, *"Absolutely. You know I will. I love you!"* We kissed each other good night, I turned on my music, and we both drifted off to sleep.

Chapter 19: Let's Get Moving – A Commitment to Building Strength

Tuesday, March 3, 2015

In this new hospital room, we had less people in and out during the night. They tried to allow Paul to get as much uninterrupted sleep as possible. I was very thankful for that because it also meant I was able to get a few hours of uninterrupted sleep...and I didn't have to feel guilty about it. That sleep allowed me to be a better wife, mother, daughter, sister, friend, etc.

It was around 6:00am when the tech came in to take Paul's vitals. It felt like we had slept for 10 hours straight even though it was more like 5-6 hours.

As I was getting up and ready for the day, Paul looked over at me and asked, *"Are you still willing to marry me?"* I looked back into his handsome eyes and said, *"Of course I am! I love you and I am so very thankful for you!"* We hugged each other for a couple of minutes and realized just how blessed we were to have this time together. I knew it would take some time to fully "get over" what had happened, but I forgave Paul. That forgiveness was for the both of us. We had a lot to do, and we needed to focus on that.

While we wished we could have just spent the day together, we knew there was still a lot to do to help Paul gain his strength. Paul ordered breakfast and was ready to start his day. Physical Therapy (PT) and Occupational Therapy (OT) would be in soon. The day prior, PT had been in briefly trying to get Paul to sit up on the side of the bed. He couldn't last thirty seconds on his own strength. They assumed he would need a lot of help to get him stronger. Here was my morning update:

March 3rd – Morning Report:
UPDATE: Praising God for such a great morning!

Paul was able to get some restful sleep last night without the need for heavy medicine. They gave him a little melatonin and he slept for a few hours – Hallelujah!

He is awake and in great spirits! While he still has more to do for recovery, we will tackle it together - one step at a time!

He has started to read some texts and messages - I should not have given him his phone. While there are still some foggy details, overall, he is back with us!

Today will be another big day. He ordered breakfast. And, while disappointed he cannot have cereal yet, he can at least have some oatmeal & milk!!

He will have Occupational & Physical Therapy today. They also pulled his labs so we will see how those look. Praying for continued improvement.

We truly have a loving, amazing, all-powerful God! He has performed a miracle in waking Paul up and giving him a happy and thankful spirit! God has special plans for Paul! I am so very excited to watch those unfold!

More to come later today. Just truly grateful for all of your support & prayers!

With that update, we started our day. Paul was able to get his breakfast. While it wasn't what he had hoped to eat, he was thankful for real food. We weren't able to bring any outside food for him as the nutritionists were watching his intake per each meal and the totals each day. There were several specific items they were monitoring. And, even though he moved from the clear liquid menu to the full liquid menu, there were still some things he couldn't eat and others were only in limited portions. I realized I would have so very much to learn about his new diet before we went home. But, for now, I was thankful they were doing that work.

We waited for PT and OT to arrive. Both arrived later in the day. I was thankful they were there, and was hoping to get on a schedule with them – to have specific days and times they would be there to work with Paul. It was several days since I had been home to see our little ones. I wanted to know when Paul would be occupied with other things so I could plan quality time to be home with the kids. Paul wasn't ready to have the kids come up yet, so we had just talked with them through FaceTime. I really needed some mommy snuggle time.

While I wanted a more clearly defined schedule, I learned that wasn't possible. The PTs and OTs would get their list of patients each morning and try to see them during the day. Considering that each patient's day was different, there wasn't a way to put together a schedule. They would just stop by, and if the patient wasn't available, they would move onto the next patient and try to make it back by before the end of the day. While I was hoping there was some way to have a more structured schedule, that wasn't going to be possible. So, I needed to let it go. Regardless of when they came, I needed them to be happy and focused on Paul getting better. I knew Paul's mood would continue to improve as he regained his strength. So, I would need to find another time to get back home to be with the kids.

We learned a few additional things from the PT. One, the yellow socks on Paul's bed were noting that he was a "fall risk" and he could not get out of bed without a hospital staff member. Considering Paul could barely sit up for thirty seconds the day prior, this didn't seem to be an issue. That was until the PT was able to get Paul standing with a walker! Praise God! Paul couldn't walk far, but he was able to stand and move a little bit. That was great progress in just twenty-four hours!

We were again reminded that it would take at least three days of extra strength building for every one day Paul was in the ICU, plus extra time for him in the medical unit when he wasn't moving very much. So, the more Paul did to build his strength, the less time it would take to get him back to normal – or at least to whatever his new normal would be. Paul asked the PT if he thought Paul would be able to play basketball again. The PT was encouraged by his progress and felt like this was a likely possibility – but it was going to take Paul time and it would be a lot of work to get there.

With all of that news, Paul wanted the PT to ditch the yellow socks and take him off of "fall risk" so he could get moving.

He wanted to do whatever he could to regain his strength ASAP, so he didn't want to wait for the hospital nurses and staff. Of course, the PT wasn't going to let that happen, but he was encouraged by Paul's positive attitude, and so was I.

We were also so thankful that the pulmonologist who was on Paul's service over the weekend stopped by. Even though he was no longer on Paul's service, he still wanted to see how Paul was doing. He encouraged us to have the kids come up to see Paul. He felt it would be good for everyone. Paul wasn't ready for that yet. He said, *"maybe tomorrow"*, but I could see in his eyes that he didn't mean tomorrow either. It was tough enough to talk with them on FaceTime. They had questions he didn't have the answers to. He wanted them to see him healthy again, not sick in a hospital bed. He wasn't ready.

He also wasn't ready to have friends visit either. Several friends asked him if they could stop by, but he told them not to come. He always had a reason why they shouldn't visit, but I think the true reason was that he didn't want others to see him this way. Since we didn't have any pictures, he didn't understand his progress. He couldn't grasp that people had already seen him so sick, and seeing him now would be amazing! They would be able to see the miracles that God had provided with their own eyes. Paul wasn't ready to accept that yet. He was still sick.

He wasn't himself. He didn't want anyone to do anything extra for him. He didn't want to be a burden. I tried to talk with him about this, but I figured we didn't need to push the issue today. He was awake. We would have more time. We didn't have to do all of this today. Here was my evening post:

> **March 3rd – Evening Report:**
> UPDATE: Amen. Amen. Amen!
>
> Paul is resting comfortably - and this time I truly mean that!! He finished dinner, took his evening meds - Benadryl & melatonin, and is now drifting off to a good sleep.
>
> Lungs - he still has his nasal cannula. They are weaning him off the oxygen support. While he could probably do it on his own, I like the additional reassurance that it is on.
>
> Kidneys - still need prayers here. His creatinine was over 9 yesterday and just down to 8+ this morning. Tomorrow morning's labs are important. The hope is that they stay the same or go down as he had some urine output. Everyone believes his kidneys will bounce back - we just don't know how long that will take.
>
> Paul will undergo another 3.5 hour hemodialysis tomorrow with the goal to both clean the blood and to pull off additional fluid. They will not allow anyone else in that room, so please also pray Paul handles that time well. I have been by his side through almost everything since he woke up. We are charging his phone so he will have that with him. Praying for a good experience for him.
>
> Strength - Paul had PT today and stood up for the first time - Praise God!! He is more able to move around in his bed, which is also great news. He is ready to walk to the bathroom;

> however, his legs truly aren't ready for that. While his mind says he can, his body says not yet.
>
> Spirit - overall, Paul is in pretty good spirits! He loves reading the posts, texts, etc. While many of them make him a little misty, he truly feels the love, support and prayers you have filled us with throughout this journey. Thank God for all of you!!
>
> Kids - we were able to FaceTime the kids a few times which is good for everyone. We will see when we can bring the kids up. Maybe tomorrow, depending on dialysis & therapy. Need to get those pictures back up on the walls as I took them down from ICU and haven't replaced them yet :).
>
> Thank you again for joining us on this journey! Praising our amazing God for another day of progress. Praying for another good day tomorrow.

After that post, Paul and I were alone in the room, talking about the day. I realized that I hadn't fully shared the news about my job with him. He had an idea of what was going on, but with everything else he was dealing with, I didn't give him all of the details. So, we spent some time talking about the details. What was surprising to both of us is how at peace we both were with the situation. While I didn't know what I would do moving forward, we were handling the news pretty well...*at least we thought we were.*

I also knew I hadn't shared this update with our family and friends. The posts had all been about Paul, about his health, about his progress, about specific prayer requests, and thankfulness for all of the love, support and prayers. None of this had been about me...it was all about Paul, and God's miracles. That said, people kept asking about me. My answer would always revert back to how Paul was doing. My health, my wellbeing was wrapped up in Paul's health. I really didn't have anything else to share...until now. Paul encouraged me to share the news. Here was that post:

> **In other news ...job loss ...**
>
> Well, I thought I would add this because I could truly use some prayer support myself. I found out yesterday that I will be losing my job. We were going through a corporate realignment and my position was eliminated. I have a couple of options:
>
> 1- I can look for other positions within the organization.
> 2- I can take severance (which is truly a very good deal) and seek employment elsewhere.
>
> I have been at the same organization for 16.5 years and it has been a truly great experience! In that time, I have had 8 different positions and moved up the corporate ladder fairly quickly.
>
> I am just praying for God to help me make the right decision. Your additional prayer support for that is greatly appreciated.
>
> Please know I am truly at peace and hold no ill feelings toward my organization. I have done good work and they have paid me well - it was a great partnership.
>
> I am wondering if this is another God moment. Is He telling me it's time to move on? I will share this - with everything going on with Paul, I truly feel at peace in this current situation. Surprisingly, this has had very little effect on my spirit. Watching Paul progress helps me keep everything in perspective. Praising God for that!
>
> Thank you all for your prayers. I will keep you updated on this journey, too!

In retrospect, there was a lot of information I didn't share in this post. People reading it didn't know that I had known my job was up for potential elimination. They didn't know that I had been preparing for this for years, and more specifically the previous six months. They couldn't hear the sadness in my team leader's voice when he shared the news. And, they couldn't see the relief on my face when I looked into my husband's eyes and saw our future. If God could save Paul, He can do *anything*. He had a plan for us. It was up to me to be patient and obedient to that plan. Right now, that plan included taking care of Paul.

With that, it was time for Paul and I to try to get some sleep. The next day was going to be a big day. We were going to see what the labs looked like to better understand what was going on with his kidneys. That would determine whether or not Paul needed to go to dialysis. We assumed he would need to go, but we were hopeful for good numbers. Regardless, we needed to get some sleep.

Before going to sleep, I asked Paul if we could read the daily devotional from *Jesus Calling* together. I was going to read it, and go back the few days that I had missed. He agreed, so I opened my app to February 27th. I read the devotionals from the 27th to March 3rd. Considering all we were going through, the messages – again – could not have been more perfect.

After reading the devotionals, I asked Paul, *"Will you marry me?"* He replied, *"Everyday!"* We kissed goodnight and rolled over to sleep...while listening to what was now becoming "our" music.

Chapter 20: This is God's Story

Wednesday, March 4, 2015

When I woke up on Wednesday, Paul was already awake. He had a hard time staying asleep during the night, so he opened up his phone. He started reading some of the messages from everyone – which was amazing and also had his head spinning. He still didn't fully grasp all that had happened, all who had already been up to see him, and all the prayers, love and support from everyone. It was a lot to take in, so as you can imagine, it was difficult to get back to sleep. I was again kicking myself for giving him his phone.

When I looked at Paul, I could see he was starting to process what had happened. I asked him, *"How are you doing? Are you okay? That was a lot to take in. How can I help?"*

Paul looked back and answered, *"I am not sure. I have a lot of questions, but I don't know that I am ready for the answers. Just please tell me that you will never leave me. I need you. Please say you will still marry me."*

I jumped up and wrapped my arms around Paul. I told him, *"I am not going anywhere! I love you, and I am so thankful that God gave me you – and that He brought you back to me. I am here to answer your questions whenever you are ready."*

He wasn't ready to get into any of the details yet, so we tabled that conversation for a later time. We were waiting for the lab results and for Paul's breakfast to arrive. I helped him get ready, as we assumed this would be a dialysis day. Again, we were still hoping for good numbers.

I was also looking forward to spending some time with our little ones. It had been a long time since I was able to get some good mommy-snuggle time. And, now that Paul was awake and improving, I had real positive news to share with them. They didn't understand just how bad their daddy was; they just knew he was getting better and able to talk with them. That was good enough for them.

There was a knock at the door. We were hoping it was the nurse, but instead, it was the gentleman bringing up Paul's breakfast.

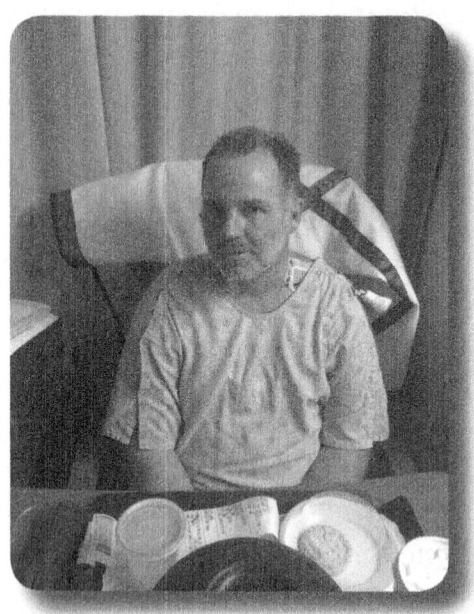

It was so good to see Paul sitting up with little help. He was holding his head up much better now, and he didn't need any help to eat. Praise God! You can see the tape from the ports and the scab on his lip from where the vent clip was rubbing. That said, you can also see his personality coming through. Look at that smirk. He was ready to take on the day!

After breakfast, the nurse came back in with the numbers. We were truly hopeful the kidney numbers would stay stable, showing the kidneys were doing some work. Unfortunately, that was not the case. Here was the update:

March 4th – Morning & Afternoon Report:

UPDATE: So sorry for the delay in the morning report. It has been a busy morning.

First, Paul cannot thank you all enough for your prayers & support. When he woke up around 1:00 am, he started reading the Facebook posts, texts, messages, etc. He is truly overwhelmed by the love you have all shared. Thank you!

Kidneys - still need prayers there. His creatinine was above 10 this morning. Again, the goal is below 1.3. While he is making urine, the kidneys haven't started filtering yet. Please pray those kidneys kick in.

PT/OT - we hope he will have the strength to do one or both today. He wants to be able to sit up in bed and stand to get to a chair. While we see his amazing improvements, he still thinks of himself as the five day/week basketball machine that he was before this started. He has made such progress thus far! Praying God provides him with patience and peace.

Diet - Paul is also advanced to a regular (renal) diet - woohoo!! He is looking forward to more options in meals. Again, clear & full liquids are better than tube feeds or ice chips which was all he could have over the weekend - but, I can completely understand his desire to eat more.

Will send an update later tonight. Thanks again for your prayers. And, thanks be to God for His miracles!!

While there were many things to be thankful for, we were also very aware that Paul's kidneys were still in need of a lot of healing. Again, in my non-medical, over-simplification of kidney function – I understand they play two key functions: (1) filtering the blood to remove unneeded/unwanted "junk" and (2) producing urine to get that "junk" out of the body. Paul had started making urine, so we were seeing that portion of the kidney function improve. He still wasn't back to normal kidney function, but it was such a significant improvement from where he was. And, we could see that improvement with every bathroom break. The challenge was the other half. The only way to know if the kidney filter had kicked in was through the lab results. And, the morning lab results were not positive. His creatinine levels were continuing to increase, so dialysis was necessary. His body needed help filtering the blood to get the "junk" out.

Before he left for dialysis, I asked if I could download the <u>You Version Bible App</u> & <u>Jesus Calling</u> from iBooks onto his phone. He was going to be in the dialysis unit for a few hours. And, while I knew he had a lot of catching up to do on Facebook & Twitter, I also wanted him to have the option to fill up on God's Word. With that, he went off to dialysis and I went home to see the kids.

I was able to spend some good time at home with the itty bittys, and I was able to have lunch with Paulie at school.

Paulie asked if we could take a selfie and send it to Dad. He wanted his Daddy to see him eating a healthy lunch – even though that might be a cookie.

It was great to be able to spend time with him at school. We spent extra snuggle time and he was able to show me his star student photo.

I was completely amazed at how our little guy was handling this entire situation. He was doing all of the right things, helping his brother and sister, and excelling in school. I'm still not sure how he was able to do all of that; just so grateful God helped him through it...when I couldn't.

I went back home and spent more time with our itty bittys, and took the opportunity to take a shower and relax for a few minutes. I grabbed some new fresh clothes in exchange for the ones I had at the hospital. I also had brought some of Paul's dirty clothes home with me. This was a big deal as it meant that he actually had dirty clothes. He was awake and alive. He was moving around. He wanted clean underwear, shorts and t-shirts for PT and OT. And, he wanted new socks, but that would need to wait a little while. He still needed his yellow "fall risk" socks until cleared by PT.

The time at home was amazing! The kids made more pictures for Paul to see when he got back from dialysis. They also asked when they could come up and see Paul. While I knew he wasn't ready yet, I felt it would be soon. In the meantime, we would continue to FaceTime to see each other, but maybe this weekend we could get together.

Another topic came up when I was home. Paul and I had discussed it a bit the night before, and it was discussed by the family quite a bit while he was "asleep". Back then, we needed to focus on him living first and improving second. Now that he was awake and alive, the topic came back up. *Should we talk with a lawyer about a lawsuit?*

What I truly appreciated about the conversations was the focus of the discussion. *What would we be looking to gain from a lawsuit?*

We knew that the doctor did what he thought was best. There was no malicious intent there. He didn't want to misdiagnose

Paul. It was an accident. And, medicine is not a perfect science. While the vast majority of the time doctors make the right decisions, there will be times when mistakes are made. I truly believed this was what happened with Paul. The doctor took in the information he had and made the best diagnosis based on that information. It is truly unfortunate that the diagnosis was wrong, but God didn't let that be the end of our story.

We also knew that we were not looking to "get rich" off of this. While it would be great to have the additional doctor bills covered, the ones we would be responsible for after insurance covered their portion, we weren't looking for anything more.

All that said, if the outcome were different, if Paul didn't survive, we would have had a different set of circumstances to consider. We would have both doctor bills and then long-term decisions about life without Paul. But, we didn't have that to worry about. Paul was here and improving.

So, we agreed to get through the next few weeks without focusing on that. We would see what insurance would cover and get a better understanding of our financial contribution. We had some stocks we could sell to help cover those costs. If we could cover the costs, we didn't want to bring a lawsuit into the mix. We just wanted Paul to heal. And, we all felt very good with that decision.

After some really great time at home, I went back to the hospital. Paul seemed to be in better spirits, although the dialysis did wear him out some. Then, the PT came by to see him. He was impressed by Paul's ability to stand and take a few steps in the room with a walker – especially after a full dialysis. While Paul wanted to do more, the PT wouldn't let him. He would still need to keep those yellow socks for a while.

And, you may remember that Paul had started losing weight early in the year and was competing in a weight loss challenge with some friends. Now that the dialysis was pulling off some of the extra fluid weight, Paul was also thinking that he might be able to win that challenge. While I am certain this was not the way he would want to win it, this did give him something to strive toward. It kept his mind focused on getting healthy, building his strength and losing weight.

It was a great day, and here was the evening report:

March 4th – Evening Report:

UPDATE: Another amazing day for Paul! Hallelujah!

Lungs - He was able to spend most of the day off of oxygen. They are monitoring him overnight without the oxygen to see how he does - Praise God for healing Paul's lungs!

Central Line - coming out tomorrow. Infectious Disease is very happy with Paul's progress. And, Paul is happy to have one more line removed from his body - Amen!

PT - Paul was able to stand & walk (with a walker). He probably could walk without the walker, but we are taking baby steps. No need to wear him out too soon. He is focused on his recovery and building his strength. Wants to still beat the boys in the weight loss challenge.

Kidneys - still needing prayers for healing. His creatinine was over 10 this morning. Paul went back to hemodialysis and did really well. Praying for those kidneys to kick in! The good news is that Paul is now consistently making urine :).

We cannot thank everyone enough for your prayers & support! We also learned that some friends have started a "GoFundMe" site as we know these hospital bills will be pretty pricey. We are truly grateful for those who have already donated. Brought us to tears!

Will send report in the morning. Thank you all again! Hope you all have a great night!

Yes, you also read that correctly. Just as we were talking about our family needs of financially covering the medical expenses, God had moved some friends to start a "GoFundMe" account on our behalf. I had been looking into our insurance portion, so I figured we would be responsible for ~$10,000 of expenses. I had not shared that information with anyone. And, there it was.

A "GoFundMe" account set up with the goal of $10,000. **What a God moment!** That helped to solidify in my mind what God wanted us to do. He had provided so many miracles in healing Paul. Now, He had provided us additional relief to us by *lifting up our community again* to help take this additional stressor away. This story was to be focused on Him, not on anything else. He had already provided so much and wasn't done yet. Truly, we have such an amazing God!

We had so very many people helping us! We had the family and friends coming to the hospital. We had so many providing meals through meal train and stopping by with groceries, food, help with the kids, etc. Now, we had a means to help cover our expenses. We could so clearly see how God was working to make this situation the best it possibly could be. It was so very much to deal with, but God had it under control…always. We just needed to keep the faith and continue to focus on our relationship with Him.

It had been a long day, and we were both very tired. I asked Paul to marry me. He smiled at me and said, *"Yes!"* It was the first time either one of us asked and it wasn't an overwhelmingly tearful moment.

We read <u>*Jesus Calling*</u> and prayed together before we drifted off to sleep. This was the very first time we specifically prayed together, at least a prayer that wasn't a typical recitation. We prayed deeply and fully. We shared our thankfulness for all God had provided. We could see how He had engaged a community to help us during this time. They were praying, they were helping, and they were doing His work. And while we knew there was still a lot of work to do, this night was focused on thankfulness…and prayers for a little extra help with the kidney filter.

Chapter 21: This is a Process – Be Patient

Thursday, March 5, 2015

While I thought we were going to get a good night of sleep... that didn't happen. Paul was struggling with staying asleep. He could fall asleep most nights, but something or someone would wake him up and then his mind would start spinning. It was flooded with a lot of thoughts and questions. And, when he was awake, he wanted the answers. I was thankful he would let me sleep some, and I was also thankful he would wake me up to help answer some of his questions. I didn't want him to be swirling. There would always be more time for sleep. I wanted to be available whenever he was ready to talk.

I thought one option was to give him a mantra – something he could repeat to keep him focused on all the positives that had happened, on all that God had already provided. The mantra was:

- God's Got this
- This setback is temporary
- Our Love is Forever

We repeated this to each other several times, and I drifted back off to sleep. Paul said he wasn't far behind.

When we woke up (or when I woke up), Paul looked pretty refreshed. He was at least ready to take on the day, and it was going to be a pretty busy one. He looked over at me, smiled and asked, *"Will you marry me?"* He had the cutest smirk on his face, so I asked, *"What is the smirk for?"* to which he replied, *"I just love you!"* We knew it would seem weird to continue asking each other this each day, but we both agreed that we wanted to do it, so we did.

Paul had a really great day. His session with OT was very productive, including a couple laps around the unit with the walker. He asked to do a lap without the walker, but that was not yet an option. It was amazing to see how much his strength had improved in such a short time. On Sunday, he could barely sit at the side of his bed for thirty seconds. Now, just four days later, he was walking around the unit. Praise God! What a miracle!

They had also been able to take the central line out of his neck. This was great news as it gave Paul another example of just how much he had already improved. One thing we didn't think about was...the nurses were pulling blood out of the central line. With it removed, they would now need to "stick" him each time to get the blood. And, Paul is not very fond of needles. *One step forward...*

The nephrologist had also come by to discuss Paul's labs. We were expecting a bigger drop in Paul's creatinine level, but it didn't happen. And, we would again need to see what the levels looked like on Friday, as that would be forty-eight hours after dialysis. The goal would be to see another decrease or at least stabilization. So, Friday's labs would be very important.

The nephrologist also told us that the two things keeping Paul in the hospital were his strength and his kidneys. He was pleased with Paul's progress on strength, and Paul had started making more urine, which were steps in the right direction. He cautioned us that most insurance companies would not allow patients to be discharged while on dialysis, so we should plan to be there for a while.

Here was my afternoon post:

March 5th – Afternoon Report:
UPDATE: Paul is still having trouble sleeping through the night. He is getting some sleep, but he hasn't had a full night sleep.

Strength - Paul was working with occupational therapy today. He did such a good job! He was taking laps around the unit and felt great! We are hoping PT will also stop by today.

Central Line - they were able to pull the central line today - Amen! One less line to worry about.

Kidneys - Creatinine is just below 9. While that is really high, the doctor was pleased with the drop. The question will be what tomorrow's labs look like. With Paul making urine, we are hoping the increase is minor.

Discharge - while Paul feels better, he is still not ready to come home. I know he was hoping to leave tomorrow; however, the doctor confirmed that is not possible. We are hoping maybe sometime next week / weekend. That would still be ~3 weeks. All considering, 3 weeks is nothing!

With all of that, the three prayer requests are:
- Kidneys
- Strength
- Patience on discharge

We truly feel the love, support & prayers! I've given Paul this mantra:
God's got this
This setback is temporary
Our love is forever

Throughout the day, we continued to get good news. He was able to spend the entire day off of oxygen and he was maintaining a fairly good oxygen level. Sometimes, when they would test him, his levels would be in the low 90s. After a few deep breaths, it would be back up near 100. It helped him to understand the importance of using the breathing apparatus the respiratory therapist provided. This would measure the amount of air he could breathe in. He was supposed to use this five to ten times an hour (I think that was the amount). He hadn't been doing it, and now he was able to see why it was needed.

We received other great news through the day on the remaining lab tests, on the ability to discontinue of some medicines, etc. Here was the evening report:

> **March 5th – Evening Report:**
>
> UPDATE: Today was another good day for Paul!
>
> - Lungs - he is completely on room air - no oxygen needed.
> - Liver, platelets, white count - all normal.
> - Done with antibiotics & steroids.
> - Only line left in him is for dialysis.
> - Rash has completely healed.
>
> Your specific prayers have been answered. I hope you can feel the power of prayer! It has worked!
>
> I received a message from a neighbor who has been praying with his daughter for Paul. When he told her Paul was doing better, she said **"Wow! I think our prayers worked!"** Yes, they did! They really did!
>
> Tomorrow - we will see what Paul's labs look like. He will likely need hemodialysis tomorrow and will not likely be discharged before mid-week next week. This will allow him to get stronger and allow the doctors to watch his kidneys.
>
> As I lay here next to Paul, I am truly thankful. I am thankful for all of you! And, I am thankful for God's decision to bring Paul back to us. Fourteen days ago, we were in the ICU praying for Paul to live. Tonight, I kissed him goodnight. We have the rest of our lives together & we will be thankful for every minute; we know tomorrow is not guaranteed.

As I have stated previously, I had gotten many comments about how people were praying differently than they had prayed before. They were not just praying more deeply, they were also seeing the immediate answer to very specific prayers. They shared that this experience helped them to see God and Jesus in a completely new way. Every time I read one of these messages, I would break down in tears and thank God – not just for the healing of Paul, also for the privilege to share His story with others and help them to gain a new and/or possibly a deeper relationship with Him.

Another blessing was that several of our friends had shared Paul's story with their children, and they were praying alongside their children for God's healing of Paul. So, as Paul continued to improve, the children were able to see how their prayers could be answered. I must say, when our friend shared this with us about his daughter's reaction to Paul's healing, I fully broke down in tears. I was overwhelmed that God was using Paul's healing as a way to also help little ones see His desire for a deeper relationship. *Praise You, Lord!*

As we prepared for sleep that night, I asked Paul to marry me. This put a smile on both of our faces. While we knew we would get used to this, it still seemed a little awkward. He agreed to marry me, and we settled in together.

We read *Jesus Calling* and prayed very deeply and specifically together. We thanked God for another amazing day. We recounted the many blessings of that day and prayed for specific improvements for the next day. We also thanked God for blessing us with the opportunity to share His Amazing Grace with so many through Paul's journey. This really was God's story, and we were overwhelmingly grateful that we had the opportunity to share it with so many others through both direct connection and social media.

Chapter 22: One Step at a Time

Friday, March 6, 2015

We had both gotten some pretty good sleep, and there was very little activity in the room that night. When the technician came in to take Paul's labs, we had been sleeping for a good 5-6 hours. Our best night sleep yet!

While we waited on the lab results, Paul ordered his breakfast and we started getting ready for the day. As I was helping Paul get dressed, he looked up and innocently asked, *"Will you marry me?"* This time there was no smirk, and it was less awkward and full of sincerity. I think I blushed at the way he asked the question. I smiled back and said, *"Absolutely! I thought you would never ask."*

I finished helping Paul get ready, he ate his breakfast and we waited on the lab results. When we got the news, we were more than disappointed. He had been making more urine, so we were so hopeful that his labs would show his kidneys had "woken up" and they were clearing more. Unfortunately, that was not the case, and his creatinine level was the highest to date. The numbers were so high, the nephrologist shared that Paul would be going to dialysis both Friday and Saturday. He shared that he didn't want Paul to wait two days between dialysis sessions as the numbers could become critical and he didn't want Paul back in the ICU for an emergency dialysis session. We definitely didn't want that either.

So, Paul went off to dialysis and I went home to see the kids. While it was never enough time, I was thankful that I had the time to come home while Paul was otherwise occupied. It gave me the peace of knowing it was okay to be away from him, and a timeframe of when I needed to be back.

Here was my afternoon update:

March 6th – Afternoon Report:

UPDATE: We are still waiting on those kidneys to wake up. His creatinine was 12 so dialysis was a must. Those are Paul's least favorite four hours of the day

Unfortunately, he will also need dialysis tomorrow to help the creatinine come down. He is not looking forward to that!

During those 4 hours, I was able to go home & hang out with our little two. Plus, I spent some time with a couple of friends (thank you for visiting!). I also went to school to have lunch with Paulie. It was great seeing all of their smiling faces!

I was able to bring Paul's Fitbit to the hospital. While we can't personally do much about the kidneys, we can focus on his strength. So, he will have that back on and we will start counting steps.

Hopefully, PT/OT will be in soon as Paul is jumping at the chance to get moving!

We also had a visit from one of the ICU doctors. He just wanted to see how Paul was progressing. We are truly blessed to continue to have such great care!

Praising God for His amazing miracles! He continues to move mountains and heal Paul's body. We pray for his kidneys to wake up, so we can all be back home as a family.

Thank you all!

There were so many things I didn't add to this update. When Paul went to dialysis, I came home to spend time with the itty bittys and see Paulie for lunch. When I got home, I knew Paul wanted me to find his Fitbit, but it was nowhere to be found. I looked everywhere. It wasn't in any of the usual places, and it wasn't in any of the random places I looked. I didn't have much time because I needed to leave to surprise Paulie for lunch – again.

Look at that smile! And, look at those missing teeth – I just LOVE this picture!

I had such a great time seeing Paulie. He was completely surprised and thankful I was able to spend more time with him. He talked with me about things going on that day, we spent time talking to his friends, and he took extra time to snuggle on me. *I needed that time.*

Before I left the lunch, I asked him if he had seen his Daddy's Fitbit. I knew Paul was really looking forward to getting that back on to see his progress each day, and I was disappointed that I couldn't find it. When I asked Paulie, he told me that he knew exactly where his Daddy's Fitbit was. It was on the shelf in Paulie's bedroom. He had seen it a few days prior, and had put it on to get his Daddy some steps. His goal was to get all five lights lit up each day because he didn't want his Daddy to lose any steps.

My eyes filled up with tears as he shared this information. I was just so very thankful that we were having this conversation.

His Daddy was awake and wanted his Fitbit. Oh, what a different conversation we could have been having. And, how seriously cute was it that Paulie was trying to get his Daddy some steps. He loved his Daddy so very much, and this was a way for him to physically show it while his Daddy was still in the hospital. Paulie would get the steps for his Daddy and light up his Fitbit! I snuggled him tightly, kissed his forehead, and thanked him for loving his Daddy so much – for loving all of us so much! *We are truly blessed!*

Sadly, lunch was over, so we snuggled again and said our good-byes. I thought I would be able to come home the next morning, as Paul would definitely have dialysis. However, I was worried about promising anything to the kids that I couldn't guarantee. While I was hoping to see the kids the next day, I didn't know how long Paul's dialysis run would be, or if I would be able to get home. So, I decided not to share this with Paulie, as I didn't want to let him down in case anything needed to change.

On my way home, I was thinking about Paul and the kids. He hadn't seen them yet. He had spent time on the phone and FaceTime, but they hadn't been able to truly see each other. And, while I knew he didn't want visitors, I felt it was important on both sides to get them together. So, when I arrived home, I talked with my sister about planning a trip to the hospital. I wasn't sure if it would be Friday, Saturday or Sunday, but I wanted them to see each other that weekend. We agreed that we would figure something out. I would wait to discuss it with Paul until it was closer to the time the kids would come up. While I knew it would be great for everyone, I also didn't want to add stress to him. So, we would see how the weekend progressed. And, I prayed we would be able to make this work.

After that, I said my goodbyes to my sister and the itty bittys and headed back to the hospital. Not long after I arrived, Paul was back in his room. I gave him his Fitbit, and he was looking for the PT or OT to start taking him on trips around the floor.

He couldn't wait to get rid of those yellow socks and be able to walk without someone from the hospital staff. That said, he wasn't fully ready to do that yet, so at least having the Fitbit would allow him to see the progress he made each day. I told him about my discussion with Paulie at lunch about getting his Daddy some steps. That brought tears to Paul's eyes, and we both broke down. This moment was never guaranteed. In fact, there were so many who believed this moment was a complete impossibility. *But, with God, nothing is impossible!*

The afternoon was filled with visits from PT, OT and doctors. While they were impressed with his progress, they still wouldn't allow him to be off of "Fall Risk".

After that, several friends and neighbors stopped by unannounced. I watched Paul as he talked with our friends. It was really tough at first. He didn't know what to say, he was thankful they were there, but sad they were seeing him that way. He never wanted to be a burden or put anyone out. He would tear up for the first few minutes they were there, but then it was like old times. We would all get into other conversations that were easier for everyone to handle. I could see Paul ease into the discussions, and after they left, he was thankful they stopped by. He still felt like he was "putting them out" but was grateful they were willing to take time to come and see him. Right then I knew, we needed to get the kids up there soon...before he changed his mind. He was too tired today, but tomorrow was likely the day.

I had also been getting some messages from other friends wanting to come up. When they sent a note to Paul, he would tell them not to come up. However, when other friends just showed up, it was a rough few minutes, but then Paul was thankful to see them. So, I shared these stories with them and told them to stop asking. If they asked, he would say *"no"*. If they just showed up, he wouldn't have anything to say.

> ***Note:*** *As I am writing this, I know it may seem like such a terrible thing for me to do. Paul wanted his space and didn't want others to see him this way. That said, he still couldn't grasp the number of people who had already seen him, or knew what was going on through the blog and Facebook posts. They were already invested in his recovery, and they wanted to see Paul awake. Plus, when Paul talked with the friends and neighbors that afternoon, I saw how much he appreciated the effort. He wouldn't ask or approve of anyone coming – if it were up to him. But, if people came on their own, he would not send them away. So, I felt it was the right thing to do – on both sides.*

We had a full day and got ready for bed. I was able to walk him to the bathroom for the first time. The nurse helped me get him in there, and then I ran up the hall to the public restroom to get myself ready for bed.

> ***Note:*** *I guess I haven't shared that the bathroom in the patient's room is for the patient only. So, I would have to use the public restroom down the hall to get ready for bed. While it wasn't convenient, it was manageable. I would run down the hall each night before bed to wash my face, brush my teeth, take my contacts out, etc. I would run back to Paul's room, as fast as I could, because I knew he still didn't like to be alone. But, as a "rule follower", I was completely fine with doing whatever was necessary to be able to stay with Paul.*
>
> *The only thing that was more difficult was going to the bathroom in the middle of the night. I get up each night at least 1-2x to go to the bathroom. So, every night, I would wake up, put my socks on, and run down the hall a couple of times to go to the restroom. When I would get back to the room, it would take me a good thirty minutes to fall back to sleep. But, I got used to that, too. It didn't matter what I had to do. Paul had*

already been through so much. He would do anything to be able to get up by himself and go to the bathroom. Who was I to complain about running down the hall? At least I could run, by myself, down the hall. He needed help to even get out of bed. It put everything into perspective.

CHAPTER 23: TIME FOR A VISIT WITH OUR LITTLE ONES

Saturday, March 7, 2015

When we woke up, we both had a really good sleep again. Before getting started with our morning, Paul looked over at me and asked, *"Will you marry me?"* and I said, *"Yes!"* The more we asked each other, the easier it was to ask. Plus, it still made us both smile as we asked and answered the question. I stopped and prayed that we would continue this every day, for the rest of our lives.

As we prepared for the day, we knew Paul would need to go to dialysis again this morning. We were still looking forward to seeing the labs to know how well the dialysis was able to clear his blood from the day prior. Well, at least I was looking forward to seeing the labs. He didn't care about the numbers, he was just hoping for improvement.

When we saw the lab numbers, we were excited! His creatinine dropped 4 points to 8. That was the biggest drop we had seen. And, with the dialysis again the 2nd day in a row, we were hoping this would help the kidneys not have to work so hard. So, while we knew he would need dialysis again today, we were thankful for the results.

Seeing those results, and seeing how Paul had been handling dialysis, I asked him if he would be up for seeing the kids later in the day. It had been sixteen days since they had last seen each other. Now that Paul was doing better, I hoped it was time to have them come up. Plus, my entire family was in town for the weekend, and everyone wanted to come up to see Paul. They had all been very patient and respectful of his desire to not have many people at the hospital. So, even though they were in town the previous weekend when Paul first woke up, they didn't come to the hospital that Sunday or Monday.

They knew it was best for Paul to rest and heal. While they were willing to wait longer, they truly wanted to see and talk with Paul. They were all praying so deeply for him to wake up, to get better, to completely heal. While he wasn't completely healed yet, his recovery was already miraculous. They wanted to see him.

Before he left for dialysis, I told him about my conversation with my sister the day before. I wanted him to know that I hoped the kids and my family would be able to come up that afternoon. I would ask them to wait for a few hours after dialysis. He hadn't had dialysis two days in a row, so we weren't sure how he would handle it. That said, he had handled each dialysis treatment pretty well. And, they were progressively getting easier to handle. So, I was hopeful he would handle the treatment well today, and he would be able to see everyone this afternoon. He agreed!

I tried to stop the tears as I thought about the kids seeing their Daddy for the first time in over two weeks. He definitely looked sicker than they last saw him, but at least he was alive and awake and they could see him. Hallelujah!

So, Paul went off to dialysis and I added this update:

March 7th – Morning Report:

UPDATE: Paul had a really good night and he had great sleep.

Kidneys – yesterday morning, his creatinine was 12, so we knew he needed dialysis. The nephrologist wanted him to also have dialysis today as he didn't want Paul to go two days without it. This morning, his creatinine was down to 8! And, his dialysis went very well – they were able to remove another 6lbs of fluid – Amen!

His strength is improving, as is his spirit. He is looking forward to seeing the kids today. He has FaceTimed with them, but this time, he will actually see them! Praise God!

> We also want to thank everyone for the cards, notes, food, "GoFundMe" donations & prayers! We are overwhelmed by your support & generosity! We are Blessed Beyond Belief!

That's right, they were able to remove another 6lbs of fluid! He was starting to look more like the Paul who arrived at the hospital more than two weeks prior. And, he was open and willing to see the kids. *What a true blessing!*

My family came to the hospital later that afternoon and brought the kids with them. It was hard for the kids to see Paul so sick. He was their Dad, but he still looked very sick. They didn't like the feel of the hospital or the fact that their Daddy still looked so weak. It took them a while to come into the room. They stood outside and looked in, but didn't want to come in. After they did finally come into the room, they slowly walked up to the bed, and kept a little distance. Noah asked, *"Dad, are you still sick?"* Paul, with a tremble in his voice replied, *"Yes buddy, but I am getting better."*

After about ten minutes of getting more comfortable in the hospital room, they were all in his bed, snuggling on their Daddy! Paul was both amazingly thankful and overwhelmingly tearful. It took so much to hold back the tears while they were there. He didn't want them to see him cry. He didn't know how he could explain it to them. He was so very close to never having the opportunity to snuggle on them again. There aren't words to describe the emotions of that moment.

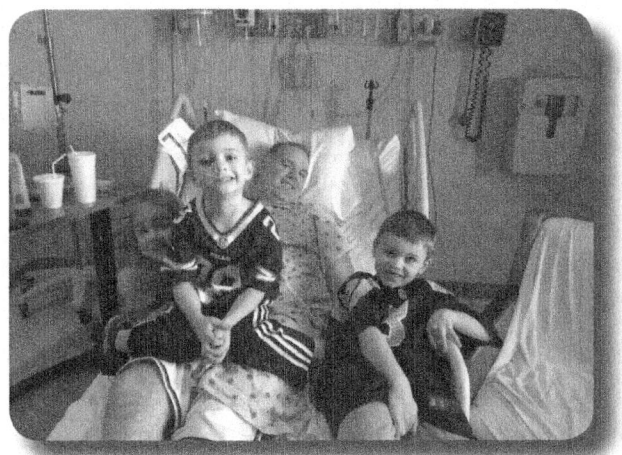

Here is a picture of Paul with Sarah, Noah & Paulie (kids from left to right)

Unfortunately, the moment didn't last long. The kids were still uneasy about being in a hospital. They also didn't like seeing their Daddy looking so weak. While they were happy to see him and know that he was alive and improving, they wanted to leave the hospital. So, after about an hour, they all left. Even though it was difficult, it was a great step forward for everyone in my family.

As we prepared ourselves for bed that night, we spent time reflecting on the day. Paul had a great set of lab numbers. Things seemed to be moving in the right direction there. Paul was able to spend time with our kids, my family and his family – plus, many friends throughout the past forty-eight hours. He had been able to handle that and had enjoyed the time spent with them. Plus, as shared in the post, we were also overwhelmed by the response to the "GoFundMe" account. We were already overwhelmed by the food via "mealtrain" and the cards, notes, gift cards, prayer requests, etc. Now, people were sending us money through this account to help with the medical bills. *Praise The Lord!* We were so very humbled by all of this. We were so very thankful, and we didn't know how we could ever thank and repay everyone for all they had done. Overwhelmed and amazingly thankful doesn't accurately describe how we felt. Not sure we can come up with words for the way we felt.

We prayed together. We gave thanks to God for all of the miracles He had already provided. We prayed that everyone would know just how thankful we were for each and every person who had taken part in this journey. We were also so very thankful for each other. We prayed for a good day of activity on Sunday and for even better lab numbers on Monday. We opened up *Jesus Calling* and read the daily passage together.

When we finished, I asked Paul to marry me and he said, "*Yes!*" We again turned on "our" music and went to sleep.

Chapter 24: A Healing Body and Swirling Mind

Sunday, March 8, 2015

When we woke up on Sunday morning, we felt very rested. We both had a great night sleep, and Paul was ready for the day. Paul had his morning lab draw, ordered breakfast and asked me to help him get ready. He wanted to walk around today and gain as much strength as he could.

When his breakfast arrived, he was sitting up waiting for them. He was committed to get moving! About half way through his meal, he looked over and said, *"Did I ask you to marry me yet this morning?"* I smiled and replied, *"Not yet, but the answer is still the same. Of course I will marry you!"* We both giggled and Paul finished his breakfast.

A few moments later, the nurse returned with Paul's lab results. Here was the update:

> **March 8th - Day Report:**
>
> UPDATE: Paul had the best night sleep thus far! He woke up with an appetite and wants to run around the hospital! Praise God!
>
> Kidneys – his creatinine did come down a bit more to 7.5. Since he has dialysis two days in a row and the first day had such a great drop, I am not sure what we were to expect. He is making more urine which is good news.
>
> Strength – Fitbit on and he is walking! He already has 1000+ steps today and is waiting on me for another walk around the unit. Hallelujah!

> Blessed — we truly cannot thank everyone enough. We truly are overwhelmed by all the love, support & prayers. Much love to you all!!

We really didn't know what to expect. When Paul was on the slow, continuous dialysis, his creatinine had dropped to 4. I must admit, I was thinking that might happen after the two days of dialysis. Unfortunately, that was not the case, which was why I should have left the expectations up to God and the doctors. That said, we were able to see the increase in urine output, and that was very encouraging. So, we were still very hopeful his kidneys would kick in sometime soon.

We were also very excited to see how well Paul was moving around. This was Day Eighteen. On Day Eleven, Paul could barely sit up on the side of the bed without falling over. Just one week later, Paul was taking laps around the unit. By 10:30am, Paul had already taken over 1000 steps!

Here is a photo of Paul after one of our laps around the unit. He has his "thumbs up" as he was feeling really great after the walk!

And, since this photo is not in color, you cannot see that Paul was able to get rid of those yellow socks!! They gave him gray socks meaning that he was no longer a "Fall Risk". He was now able to walk around the unit without medical staff. *Praise God! What a true blessing!*

We were able to spend the rest of the day with many family members and friends who stopped by to visit. It had become easier for Paul to see visitors and understand their desire to see him. It still wasn't easy, but it was easier than before.

We were also able to take some additional laps around the unit. Paul's goal was to get to 10,000 steps. We knew that was a bit of a stretch on the first day in gray socks, but it was still a good goal. We started with laps around the unit. Later, we received "off floor" privileges, so we went down to the first floor and walked around the chapel and gift shop. It was great for Paul to see sights other than his room. He was so very happy to also be able to do this on his schedule – and not have to "bother" others to help him. What made him truly happy was being able to use the restroom without help. Amen to that!

After a long day, we were getting ready for bed. We were talking about the previous week in the non-ICU room, and just how much of a routine it had become. The weekends were filled with lots of activity with friends and family, but the weekdays were pretty much the same. While we were ready for another week, we just didn't know how many more of these weeks we would be in the hospital. While we were thankful for all of the progress, there wasn't an end in sight. And, tomorrow would start week two in this room.

> *"How many more weeks would we have to be there?*
> *When would we be able to come home?*
> *How much longer would our families be able*
> *to stop their lives to take care of us?*
> *Would we ever be back to normal – or at least close*
> *to the way we were before all this happened?"*

So many questions and truly no answers...

Monday, March 9, 2015

We woke up again pretty rested and refreshed. We were ready to focus on the needs of the day. First things first in our routine – Paul's labs were drawn, he ordered breakfast and I helped him get ready for the day. We were again hopeful that the two days of dialysis would kick start the kidney filter, but we also knew not to expect anything.

As Paul was eating his breakfast, he was so excited about getting up and moving. While we assumed this would be a dialysis day, we didn't know when he would need to leave. Until that time, he wanted to see how many laps he could get in. This was at least something new we could add to the routine. We decided to stay on the unit as we were waiting to see the doctors and get the results of Paul's blood work. During one of our laps, we saw the doctors approaching and went back into his room. Here was the update from that morning:

March 9th – Morning Report:
UPDATE: Paul had a pretty good night last night and a few really good days! He has had many visitors, which has lifted his spirits - especially our little ones!

Kidneys - Praising God for the urine output!!! They say the first step to healing kidneys is making urine & the second is the filter. So, now we are praying for complete healing which means the filter kicks in.

Strength - Paul walked over 4000 steps yesterday! He also got off-floor privileges so we went around the hospital, including chapel. So grateful for all of these improvements!

Discharge - we learned this morning that Paul cannot be discharged until his kidney function (filter) is stable. The

> numbers do not need to be perfect, just stable. Then, we can move to outpatient care.
>
> Please continue to pray for kidneys - specifically for the filter to kick in.
>
> You are all amazing!! Thank you for your love, support & prayers! God is always good! And, we are forever thankful!

We were so thankful for the urine output. With that and the two days of dialysis, we were hopeful for good lab numbers. Unfortunately, his kidneys were still not functioning, so he would be heading back to dialysis. The good news was that Paul was in good spirits. While he didn't want to spend four hours in dialysis, he knew it was what was needed. Plus, he knew this would help to take off some of the excess fluid.

The other thing we had confirmed with the doctors was that insurance usually did not allow patients with acute kidney injury to be discharged to an outpatient dialysis facility. For chronic kidney disease, patients could be discharged to an outpatient facility; however, the preference was to keep patients with acute injury in the hospital for closer monitoring. That meant that we truly needed the kidneys to start filtering again. This would be a necessary step before allowing us to go home. After our discussion the night before, this wasn't great news. Paul would do everything in his power to eat the right food and get exercise. The rest was up to God healing his kidneys. Until then, we would be stuck in this routine...

Late that morning, the gentleman came to take Paul to dialysis. I was able to go home, see my sister and spend time with our itty bittys. While I would have loved to see Paulie for lunch, I didn't get home in time due to Paul's later trip to dialysis. The good news was, I got Paulie off of the bus, and spent some time with him before heading back to the hospital. Being able to spend quality time with the kids every other day had become a routine I was getting used to. Even though I wanted more time, I could only imagine how hard it was for Paul not even getting the few hours I was. I realized how blessed I was to have this time, and kept focused on making the most of every moment.

When I returned to the hospital, Paul was already in his room. The dialysis machine had clotted near the end of his treatment, so they decided not to restart it. *So much for me making it back before he was done...*

We had dinner and I filled him in on the stories from home. He was able to FaceTime with the kids, and listen to their stories first hand. These calls never lasted very long, but they were good for both Paul and the kids. They could see that Daddy was continuing to improve and were hopeful that he would be home sometime soon.

We finished the day with a few laps around the unit before getting ready for bed. While we had so many reasons to be thankful, I could see Paul truly wanted to get out of the hospital. Our discussion Sunday night and the information from the doctor today all pointed to a much longer stay at the hospital. Paul was trying to stay focused on the positives, the progress, the blessings, but he was also starting to become overwhelmed by the situation at hand:

How much longer will I be in here?
When will I be able to get back to my life?
Will I ever be back to who I was? Ever?

Chapter 25: From Frustration to Focus – God's Got This!

Tuesday, March 10, 2015

When we woke up on Tuesday, Paul was even more determined to get moving. He wanted to be active and I needed to be there with him...every step of the way.

I was very thankful for this time with Paul. We spent so many hours together talking with each other. I think we ran out of things to talk about. Especially because we were in such a routine, our lives had become pretty boring.

I also realized that, because our lives had become pretty repetitive, I hadn't been adding as many updates. For the past twenty days, we had a community of family and friends continuously praying for Paul. We were so very thankful for everything. I wanted show everyone just how many miracles God had provided as specific answers to their prayers. Here was that post:

> **March 10th – Daily Update:**
> UPDATE: Thank you all for your continued checking in on Paul's progress!
>
> We pray today is a stable day. Paul had dialysis yesterday, so his kidney numbers came back down. The prayer is that they stay down tomorrow. That is the big day to show if the filter is kicking back in. Please pray for Paul's kidneys - specifically for that filter!
>
> *Father,*
>
> *You have already performed many miracles in the healing of Paul.*

You have healed his mind. You have healed his heart. You have healed his lungs.

You have healed his liver. You have increased his strength. And, You have started healing his kidneys.

Father, I am praying boldly that You please provide complete healing for Paul. And, if I can be so bold, I pray You please place Your hands on his kidneys today and finish the healing You have already started.

God, I know You have a plan for Paul. I know Your plan, Your will and Your timing is always perfect. So, please also help us continue to come to You in thanksgiving for all You have already provided and with patience for the healing yet to come.

In Jesus' Name,
Amen!

I felt called to write that post because many people had continued to comment on my relationship with God. As mentioned previously, so many had shared their prayers were deeper, more specific, and more personal than they had ever prayed before. They were feeling a deeper connection with God while praying for Paul. So, I wanted them to see the progress through a prayer we were saying that morning.

Look at all the miracles God had provided in a short twenty days! Less than three weeks ago, we didn't know if Paul would take another breath. We focused on seconds, then minutes, then hours. Now, it has been just under three weeks, and look at all God has done! Praise Him!

After my post, we settled into our day. We were thankful for the good lab numbers this morning, but we knew Wednesday's results would again be the true indicator of Paul's kidney function. So, we focused on what we could see and what we could control. We took laps around the floor and even got down to the cafeteria that afternoon. Paul was drinking lots of water to help flush his kidneys, and we continued to see more urine output. That was all that was in our control.

We continued our daily and nightly routine. Paul's anxiety and desire to get home increased each and every day. Now, it was just a waiting game. Waiting on the kidneys to fully wake up. Waiting on that filter to start doing it's job. Waiting – patiently waiting.

My prayer that night was, *"Please God, please help Paul stay patient, thankful and prayerful. Please keep his eyes and mind on You. You have already done so very much. You have provided so many miracles to get us to this place. While we cannot know when this part of the journey will end, You do. Please help him. And, please help me. We love You and we thank You!"*

Wednesday, March 11, 2015

When we woke, Paul was definitely more anxious. He really wanted to get home to the kids. He was feeling stronger and was able to walk more than four miles the day before. The only thing holding him back was his kidney function – and he was doing all he could do to help that. He felt like he could do all of this at home and go to an outpatient dialysis center for treatments. He didn't understand why he needed to stay at the hospital. He would promise to do it all at home. He just wanted to be discharged...now!

We paced around the unit as we waited for the doctors to arrive and share the news on his labs. It seemed to be taking longer than usual. Considering Paul's emotional state, this made it even more difficult to wait. However, when they arrived, we learned more about the reasons for their delay. Here was the morning report:

March 11th – Morning Report:

UPDATE: Paul truly wants to go home. It is tough being here for three weeks. He misses our little ones and his normal routine. He misses his strength (although, he did get 8,000+ steps yesterday).

Kidneys: he is making lots of urine. I mean LOTS of urine. That is the good news.

The difficult news is that his creatinine continues to rise two days post dialysis. So, we assumed he was going back to dialysis this morning as his creatinine went up from 7.7 to 10.4. But, you have heard what happens when you assume...

The doctor came in and said some of the other kidney numbers look like they might be stabilizing. So, he is taking another blood sample at 11am and determining if Paul needs a shorter dialysis today or wait until tomorrow. He believes some of the creatinine increase can also be due to all of Paul's activity.

I also asked what happens when Paul comes home, if he still needs dialysis. He was very reassuring that he does not believe this will be a long term need (no guarantees, but doesn't expect that to be the case). While I have truly felt God showing us the same thing, it is nice to have the doctors confirm that belief.

One last update - we are looking into the potential for Paul to come home before his kidneys are perfect and moving to outpatient "acute" dialysis. Insurance usually prefers inpatient dialysis, but we are checking.

So, prayers for today:
1-11am labs show improvements
2-kidney filter kicks in fully
3-if needed, we can go home and finish this in outpatient dialysis

> Thank you for your prayers! Will update when we get results of 11am draw. Might be closer to 1pm by the time we get the results.

So, this was mixed news. While we were hoping for Paul's creatinine to stay stable or go down, the doctor seemed to think that some of the increase might have been due to Paul's exercising. And, the other lab numbers were within the normal range; so taking a second set of labs would provide more information to make the best decision on next steps. We needed to ask for specific prayers for the 2nd set of labs.

We also learned more about Paul's potential long-term needs. First, we were hopeful that Paul might be able to leave the hospital sooner than later and continue dialysis in an outpatient center. While that wasn't what insurance companies preferred, the doctor was actively looking into the option.

He also shared that he didn't believe Paul would need dialysis long-term. He shared how kidneys were resilient organs, and this was an acute injury, so the hope would be that Paul's kidneys would "wake up" and start filtering again on their own. There were no guarantees, but it was something to hope for, and to pray for.

We said our prayers and continued our laps around the unit while we waited for the 11:00am labs to come back. Here was the next update:

> **March 11th – Afternoon Update:**
> UPDATE: We received the labs back. The creatinine & BUN are pretty stable from the early morning labs, which is good.
>
> That said, the potassium is higher than they like and they want to do a quick dialysis run to help correct that. So, while Paul needs dialysis, it's only a two hour run.

> The other news is that his hemoglobin & iron are both low. So, he is getting a Procrit shot every day and is now on an IV iron drip (that was a bit disappointing as he hasn't had an IV in for a few days).
>
> We know that God is amazing and He continues to work miracles in Paul. As we are nearing 3 weeks in the hospital, there are low moments. We are looking for answers where there aren't any. And, while we can see the positives, sometimes the negatives or setbacks hit harder than they should. We know this is normal. We know we are so close to full recovery. And, we know that God is always with us.
>
> Thank you for your prayers & support. We feel we are so close to the end of this "pothole" in our journey together. We just pray God fills it in soon

Again, another mixed update. His kidney levels were stable, but his potassium was too high. While he didn't need a full dialysis, he still needed a two-hour run. Better than four hours, but he was still hoping to not have to go to dialysis at all today. He also learned that he needed help improving his hemoglobin and iron. While Paul was not a fan of getting shots, he had unfortunately gotten used to them. What he was really disappointed about was the IV. He had a couple of days without any lines going into him. Now, they needed to add the IV line back so they could infuse the iron. Minor setback, but considering his emotional state, it seemed like a major one.

I finished the update and spent time with Paul before he went off to the dialysis unit. When he left, I was feeling sad. How could I be sad? God had given us so very much. We had seen Him move mountains and part seas. We had seen Him provide miracles with every improvement Paul had. This was not a time for sadness. This was not a time for disappointment.

This was a time for celebration and thankfulness. So, I decided to write out my feelings here...

March 11th – Questions???:

We have all had trials in our lives. We have had highs and lows. We have been to the tops of the mountains and to the bottom of what seems to be the lowest valleys.

I can recall numerous times, when talking to friends in those valleys, asking...
Why you?
Why does it have to be this hard?
Why have you been through so much?
When will this end for you?
You deserve a break!

And, there are times in this journey where those thoughts have come to mind - especially considering our last 7-8 months:
July 2014 - I was diagnosed with cervical cancer
September 2014 - Hysterectomy to "cure" cervical cancer
February 2015 - Paul - Toxic Shock / me - Job Loss

As I look at what we have been through, I can definitely see where the questions would come up:

Why us?
One more thing...Why?
We have been through so much.
When is this going to end?
It is then that I realize a very different set of questions:
Why not us?

No one deserves this. But, if someone is going to get it, what makes us so special to not get it?

It makes me think about the Old Testament Book of Job. And, please know - I am NOT comparing us to Job. Job was a righteous man. He had deep faith in God and followed all of His commands. We cannot compare the way we have lived our lives to the way Job lived his life. So, seeing the TOTAL LOSS that Job endured, my question is - Why not us? What would make us so special that we should not endure loss, pain, struggle? But, I also know that God is with us - every step of the way.

Isaiah 40:26-31 (GNB):
Look up at the sky! Who created the stars you see?
The one who leads them out like an army, he knows how many there are and calls each one by name!
His power is so great - not one of them is ever missing!
Israel, why then do you complain that the Lord doesn't know your troubles or care if you suffer injustice?
Don't you know? Haven't you heard?
The Lord is the everlasting God; he created all the world.
He never grows tired or weary. No one understands his thoughts. He strengthens those who are weak and tired.
Even those who are young grow weak; young people can fall exhausted.
But those who trust in the Lord for help will find their strength renewed.
They will rise on wings like eagles; they will run and not get weary; they will walk and not grow weak.

Two of my other favorite verses are (there are so many to choose from!):
Jeremiah 29:11-13
Philippians 4:6

So, our new questions are:
What are Your plans for us?
How can we use these trials to glorify You?
How can we help others see You?

While we have some low moments, we can truly see all that God has provided!
I am cured of cancer
Paul is alive and improving every day
My job situation will work itself out - right now, I need to be patient

Here are two songs that have helped us through this time:
Kari Jobe - I Am Not Alone - https://www.youtube.com/watch?v=Ow4OfW4DP9s

Matthew West - Strong Enough - https://www.youtube.com/watch?v=A8JsRxVczmQ

Father,

I come to You today in thanksgiving! You have provided and continue to provide for all of us. While I know You didn't make any of these things happen, I also know You will bring beauty out of these crises - and You already have!

Thank You for walking with us on each and every step of this journey. While others see me as strong, I know that strength comes only from You. You have shown me the steps. You have provided the path. And, You have carried me through - each and every step of the way.

> *Heavenly Father, we know You have a plan for us. We also know Your will, Your plan and Your timing is always perfect. I pray You help us keep our eyes, minds and hearts open to fully know Your plan.*
>
> *In Jesus' Name,*
> *Amen*

With that, I had a renewed spirit. In taking the time to reflect on all God had already provided, reading His Word in The Bible, and listening to amazing Christian artists, I was renewed. God had this! He has had all of it the entire time. He didn't make this crisis happen, but He would see us through it. And, if anyone was going to have to go through this, why shouldn't it be us? With God's Strength and Help, we could get through anything. He had already proven that time and time again. He had this! It was up to us to be patient, thankful and prayerful. Now, I just needed to convince Paul of that...

When Paul arrived back from dialysis, I asked him to read my post. He did and we spent some time talking through our situation. While it wasn't where we wanted to be, we needed to be patient in the process. Our lack of patience wasn't going to make the time go faster, it would just make the time seem longer and more frustrating. We had been through so much together. This was just another "bump" or "pothole" in our journey together. God had seen us through so many other trials. Why should we assume this one would be any different?

We went into the evening with a renewed spirit. While we didn't assume this would be easy, we knew that God would see us through this. We would try to help each other focus on the positives and remain patient and prayerful. We didn't know how long this journey would take or what other bumps were ahead of us. We needed to focus on one prayerful, thankful step at a time.

Chapter 26: What??? I'm Not Ready!!!

Thursday, March 12, 2015

When we woke up, we assumed it would be a typical Thursday in the hospital. Paul would have his labs drawn and order breakfast. We would then walk around the hospital until the doctors would come in to talk with us. We would then walk around some more, eat a few times, talk with family and friends who stopped by, and go to sleep.

Considering the thoughts of how the day would go, I asked Paul if it would be okay for me to go home for a little while. It had been a few days since I had been home and we were both running out of clothes. And, while Paul was able to shower or wash up at the hospital, I was not able to really do that. I definitely needed a shower!

I waited for a while that morning for the doctors to arrive, but they were still seeing other patients. We agreed that it would be okay for me to run home quickly – not knowing when the doctors would arrive. So, off I went and promised to be back as soon as possible.

It was nearly 2:00pm when I got home. I spent a little time with our itty bittys before jumping into the shower. I sent a quick text to Paul to get the update as I was packing up to head back to the hospital. Here was our exchange:

Me:
Any news yet?

Paul:
I think I'm going home...no rush!
Putting in a new cath, then
will be on a tues, thurs, sat
dialysis schedule

They will make sure new cath doesn't ooze so still probably 4 or 5 hours Discharge papers in Nurse thinks I will be gone by 6:30	
	Wow! Ok. I am over the moon excited!!! Wahoo!! Let me get ready & I will be there. So, no clothes needed. I'll get to bring you home. Awesome!
Bring bags to pack stuff	

It was then that it hit me. He was coming home, and I was unprepared. Everything was taken care of at the hospital. He had doctors, nurses, pharmacists, nutritionists, OT/PT, etc. They were taking care of everything. Now, that would be up to me. They had saved him. On February 19th, Paul wasn't supposed to last through the night. They had kept him alive for *twenty-two* days – and in a few hours, that would all be in my hands. To say I was overwhelmed is again an understatement.

"What was I going to do? What if I do something wrong? What if he survived this long and I messed it all up? God, please help me! I am not ready! I'm not prepared! Please, God! Help!"

Unfortunately (or fortunately), I didn't share any of this with Paul. When I tried to call, he didn't answer. Here is our next text exchange:

Me:
Can u talk?

Paul:
I am asking doctor to call you

Walking up now.

I'm gone

Where are you?

Cardiology

Ok

Nervous – putting me under, love you!

Love you too. Can I come there?

I didn't hear back from Paul. It was probably best that I did not talk with him, as I didn't need to add any pressure to him prior to his procedure. That said, I didn't know if the procedure was needed. They were removing the dialysis catheter from one side and adding another to the other side. While this new one wasn't permanent, it was a little safer and more secure for him to have at home.

I arrived on the unit and spoke with the nurse. While I was gone, the doctor had come up and shared that they found an outpatient dialysis center with a spot for Paul. He felt comfortable letting Paul finish his treatments via the outpatient center and their group would be following his progress. So, they scheduled this procedure and Paul was off getting it done. Unfortunately, no one talked to me during any of this. And, I felt lost. Here was my post:

- **March 12th – Discharge???**
- UPDATE: So, I guess the delay was that they are willing to discharge Paul today. While I am excited, I am also freaking out. I definitely want him home, but I don't know what to do.
- What do I look out for?
- What do I feed him?

- What can he do?
- Yesterday, he needed dialysis.
- Today, they are willing to wait until Saturday.
- I know they know what they are doing but I don't know what I am doing.
- I trust God will see us through this, but right now, I'm really freaking out!
- Please pray.

I spoke with the nurse and told her that I wouldn't approve Paul's discharge until I personally spoke with the doctor. While I knew Paul wanted to go home, I was so afraid that I would do something wrong. And, I was concerned that waiting until Saturday for dialysis would be dangerous for Paul. I knew the doctors knew what they were doing. This was their expertise. But, this was <u>*my husband*</u>. And, I almost lost him. Now, he was alive and I didn't want to be responsible for changing that outcome.

I could barely breathe. I paced around the unit until Paul returned from his procedure. Then, I continued to pace until the doctor arrived. Not only was I scared that I wouldn't be able to take care of Paul, I was upset that I wasn't involved in the decision-making.

For twenty-two days, every decision was left up to me. I mean *every* decision – big ones, small ones, all of them. I took the information I had and made the best decisions possible. I prayed through each one and felt God guiding me. And, we had arrived at a very positive outcome. Now, the biggest decision to date, I wasn't included in the discussion. The decision was made without me, and I needed to deal with it. Even though I would be the one responsible for ensuring everything was done correctly, I wasn't involved in the discussion. So, I was hurt. I was scared and I was hurt. I needed more information. I needed to breathe.

When the doctor arrived, I asked to talk with him in the hall. I shared my concern. Even if I didn't use the right words, he could see it all over me. *I was freaking out!* He reassured me that both Paul and I would be okay. And, while he felt completely secure in Paul going home, he also agreed that having a set of labs drawn in the morning would be appropriate to ensure Paul was stable enough to wait until Saturday for dialysis.

While I wasn't 100% convinced I would be able to handle this transition, I could see the doctor's confidence in Paul's stability and my ability to handle the situation. Paul was ready – regardless if I was ready or not. So, I needed to get ready. But, I just couldn't.

I walked back into Paul's room and told him about the conversation with the doctor. We would get lab work the next morning to determine if Paul needed urgent dialysis or not. We would also need to stop by the dialysis center, regardless of those lab results, to fill out paperwork so that they were ready for Paul either later that day or on Saturday.

The plans were that I would drop Paul off at home, and then I would need to go to the grocery store. Not knowing what was in the refrigerator, I had no idea what I would be able to feed him.

The nurse came into the room and provided me with lots of information on Paul's diet. While I am absolutely certain the information was helpful, I was not in the frame of mind to review it. It all seemed so overwhelming.

"What in the world is happening? Just a couple of hours ago, I left the hospital to shower, grab clothes, and come back for another night. Now, I was walking out of the hospital with my husband – completely freaking out about the possibility of hurting him. Please, God! I need You! I can't do this!"

I had prayed, we had prayed, that we would walk out of the hospital, hand-in-hand, going home to take care of our family. God had answered the prayer. We were going home. And, I was so scared and overwhelmed that I missed out on the opportunity to enjoy this significant blessing.

As I look back now, I wish I had handled myself better. I wish I had prepared myself for Paul's eventual homecoming, so that I could have better enjoyed this moment. Twenty-two days of constant prayers for this moment...*and I blew it!*

When we arrived home, the entire family was waiting for us. The kids all wanted to sit with their Daddy. They were careful with him as he still looked very weak, but they were also so excited to see him. They sat around him on the couch while I looked for something to feed Paul for dinner. Instead of prayerfully thanking God for this moment and watching the beauty of the kids seeing their Daddy back at home for the first time in over three weeks, I was flipping around the kitchen in a huff. I didn't even get one picture of this moment. And, because I was so stressed out, I don't even have a picture in my mind.

I prepared something small for Paul to eat and left for the pharmacy and the grocery store. With the diet information in hand, I walked around the store with tears streaming from my eyes. I was both worried that I might do something to hurt Paul, and overwhelmed by how terrible I reacted. I knew I needed to fix things when I got home, so I prayed God would help me find the words and the peace I needed to get through the next stage in this journey.

When I arrived back home, I broke down in tears. I apologized for my behavior and shared some of why I reacted that way – not as an excuse, as there was no excuse for my behavior. I shared my fears about taking care of Paul, more specifically, about potentially hurting him. I shared my frustration with not being included in the decision. Regardless of that, I still should not have reacted that way. And, I asked for help. We still had Paul's mom and my sister staying at the house with us. While

I knew they were willing, I specifically asked for them to help me, help us, through the next steps in this journey. I knew I needed their help. And, I wanted to let them know how much I loved them and appreciated them.

After a little more time downstairs, we all went up to sleep. This was also overwhelming as it was the first time in more than three weeks that we would be sleeping together in the same bed – in our bed. We settled in. I looked at Paul with tears in my eyes and asked, *"Are you still willing to marry me?"* With similar eyes, he looked back at me and said, *"Yes. Of course I will! I love you!"* He also let me know that he had faith in me, and in God who had brought us this far. God didn't bring us this far to let me ruin it. He would make it, we would make it, and God would make sure of it.

> **<u>Note:</u>** *Something that wasn't apparent to me at that time or for many months later was how clearly God had answered our prayers. I had asked an entire community on March 10th to pray for God to heal Paul's kidneys. I prayed **boldly** that God would finish the work He had started, fully heal Paul's kidneys and let him come home. While God's answers aren't always specific to what we ask – He very clearly allowed Paul's kidneys to be healed enough to be sent home two days later.*
>
> *So, while I **boldly** prayed for this, I wasn't prepared for God to say "Yes!" I'm not sure, even now, that I have words for that realization. Just praising God for all He has done, and continues to do – seen and unseen – for all of us.*

CHAPTER 27: BACK AT HOME – FINDING BALANCE AND A NEW ROUTINE

Friday, March 13, 2015

We woke up super early to start the day...in our own bed! We were so used to being woken up by morning labs, I guess our internal clock had been set. We knew we wanted to be at the lab by 8:00am, so we readied ourselves pretty quickly and headed off to the lab and to complete a few other errands. Here was my update:

> **March 13th - Home, Labs & Haircut!**
>
> UPDATE: Paul came home last night. While that is a complete blessing, it is also very nerve-racking. For more than three weeks, Paul has had doctors, nurses, pharmacists, techs, dietitians, etc. I was able to be his wife while these other professionals took care of him. As of yesterday, I have to take on all of those roles - the best I can with the information they gave me. And, I don't feel equipped.
>
> I was thankful the kidney doctor agreed to Paul having a blood test today to check all of his levels. I was not going to let him come home without it. So, we just had those labs done and are waiting on the results.
>
> In other good news, Paul is getting his hair washed & cut right now. He has only had a shampoo cap these past three weeks as he couldn't (and still can't) get the ports in his neck wet. So, we may be visiting the salon more often for a shampoo :)
>
> Thank you for all of your words of encouragement, support & prayers yesterday (and everyday)!

As I reread what I wrote, I had to laugh at some of my word choices. For example, *"I would not let him come home without it."* Let's be clear, I'm not sure I had that kind of control of the situation. But, this does show just how stressed out I was at that time. I was just trying to hold it together.

I was also writing this from the barbershop. Paul had not gotten his hair wet in over three weeks. While he was given a shampoo cap at the hospital, those can only do so much cleaning. They are helpful, but it's not the same as a good shampoo. So, on our way home from getting the labs drawn, we stopped in to get Paul both a much needed shampoo and haircut. Since I still wasn't in the picture-taking mood, here was Paul's selfie:

In this picture, you can start to see just how thin Paul was getting. And, you can see how he was looking stronger and more like the man that he was before he entered the hospital.

He was looking quite handsome in this picture. God gave me my husband back. He saved him. He allowed Paul to come home with me. And, if I had let Him, He would have let us walk out of the hospital, hand-in-hand. We had so very much to be thankful for, and I needed to snap out of it.

Soon after arriving home, we received a call from the doctor's office. Paul's lab values were elevated, but they were still in the safe range so we could still wait until the next day for dialysis. While some may have thought these labs were unnecessary especially considering the outcome, for my piece of mind, they were priceless.

Even though this meant that Paul didn't need dialysis until the next morning, we still needed to stop by the dialysis center to fill out all of the paperwork. While there were quite a few documents to sign, the woman helping us through the process was wonderful. She was very caring and helped explain all the papers we were signing. She walked us through the process and answered all of our questions. She also introduced us to the dietitian who provided me with different information on meal planning. Truth be told, the information the dietitian gave me was probably very similar to the information I received from the hospital. The difference was, I was in a different frame of mind and more open to receiving the information. So, while it probably said very similar things, I felt more equipped to go home and feed my husband.

When we returned home, we spent time with everyone at the house. A few neighbors had also stopped by to say hello and check in on Paul. Here was my evening update:

March 13th - Evening Report:

UPDATE: We have had a very busy & interesting day.

Paul had his labs drawn today. His creatinine, BUN & GFR are still not good, but the other numbers are looking better - so, we are waiting until tomorrow for dialysis. He will then be on a Mon-Wed-Fri schedule until his filter kicks back in.

He got a shampoo & a haircut today so he looks like my handsome husband again! That made him feel good! So glad we made the time to do that today.

> We also went to fill out all of the paperwork at the dialysis center - it was almost as much as buying a new house. We are so grateful that the nurse was awesome and put Paul at ease. And, the doctor following him there is the first kidney doctor that saw him in the ICU. We are truly blessed to have her there as she knows his entire history.
>
> While at the dialysis center, I also talked to the dietitian and she gave us great meal options. Praising God for that help as I have been STRESSED about what to feed Paul.
>
> Thank you all for your prayers & support yesterday (& every day through this journey). I truly needed them as I was feeling out of control. Since I haven't been in control of any of this, it should have been okay - but I tried to take it back. I know God has this and He will see us through. Thank you for that reminder.

As you can see in this post, I had started to see just how crazy I had been acting. I knew that God would see us through this – *He had done so much already; why should I have any doubt that He wouldn't finish the job?* I was finding the balance between controlling the pieces in my power to control and letting go of the pieces that were truly out of my hands. I needed to leave those to God. He would give us everything we needed for each day, each moment. No looking long-term into the future. No worrying about things completely out of our control. Focus on the needs of the moment, the opportunities for the day – that was where my mind needed to stay. I needed to give the rest to God. He had it anyway, and I needed to stop trying to take it from Him.

As the night was drawing to a close, we talked about the next day. Paulie was in a basketball tournament at school. Now that Paul was home, he both wanted to go and didn't want to go. He wanted to be there to support Paulie, but he didn't want to be a "spectacle" at the event. Paul was never good with situations like these. The good news was that the decision was made for him. Paul would need to leave for dialysis before Paulie's first game. So, there was no need to worry about the next day, it was taken care of.

It is amazing for me to think about how God made everything work perfectly. Instead of us worrying about the "right" thing to do, God ensured that we did what was needed. Again, no need to worry about the future – God's got that. We just needed to focus on the moment and the opportunities for the day.

On Saturday, I would drop Paul off at dialysis and be back before Paulie's first game. I would be able to talk with our friends about Paul's progress without him being overwhelmed. God took care of it. It was now time for us to rest.

Saturday, March 14, 2015

The next morning was a flurry of activity. We had been accustomed to many family members coming in for the weekend, and this weekend would be more of the same. Please know how truly thankful we were for that!

While the entire family didn't come in because they wanted to give Paul a few days to settle in, our parents and my sister's family all came in. We worked out the details of who was taking Paul to dialysis, Paulie to the basketball game, and who was staying home with the itty bittys while they slept.

I was able to drop Paul off at dialysis and make it back in time for Paulie's first game. I had the opportunity to talk with so many people who had been praying for Paul, and I was able to share that he was home and healing. Well, he was currently in outpatient dialysis, but he was out of the hospital and able to be home with us. People were amazed at Paul's progress. While there were times when it seemed like it had been forever, it had been just over three weeks. That really was no time at all.

I was also thankful that I was able to watch Paulie and his teammate win their first game! And, Paul's dad was able to bring the itty bittys with him to see their brother play!

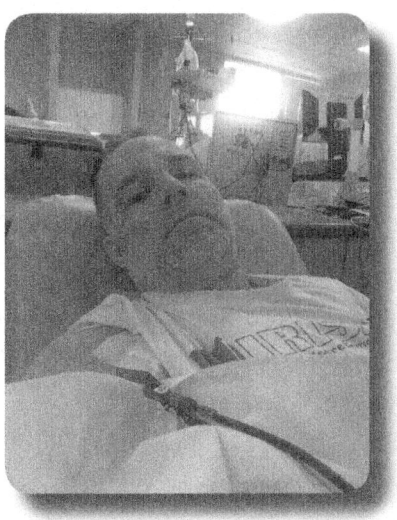

Paulie wanted his Dad to see him, so he asked me to send him this photo of Paulie hugging Noah after his first game – a winner!

Paul replied to us with this photo from the dialysis chair.

While Paul wasn't able to be at the game, he was in the place he needed to be to get better. And, while he isn't quite smiling in this photo, he did share that his experience at the dialysis center was better than expected. The people there were very nice, and everyone who was there was used to dialysis unlike the hospital where people might have been going through dialysis for the first time

Here was my morning update:

> **March 14th - Morning Report:**
> UPDATE: We have a busy morning! Paulie has a 2-on-2 basketball game. He won the first game & is having tons of fun!
>
> I have to leave here soon to pick Paul up from his first outpatient dialysis today - a 4-hour run. He isn't very excited about the 4-hours but he is happy to be home.
>
> We are getting settled into our new normal. We still aren't sleeping very well, but we are getting some sleep each night. Just so grateful we get to sleep next to each other again!
>
> Praising God for all of His miracles! Asking for one more - full healing of Paul's kidneys!

I was able to watch most of Paulie's second game before I needed to leave to get Paul. While Paulie and his teammate lost the second game, they had lots of fun. And, Paul and I were able to get home at almost the same time as the rest of the family, so Paulie was able to fill his Daddy in on all of the details of the games.

It was a great day with the family. Paul was able to stay up and talk with everyone most of the day. The dialysis took a lot out of him, but he really wanted to be with the family. He took little catnaps here and there, but was really engaged most of the time. We were all truly amazed by just how far he had come in such a short period of time. God is truly amazing!

One other thing I didn't realize was just how hard it was going to be to keep everyone updated now that we were home. At the hospital, I would have some time to myself to add the posts. Now that we were home, I didn't have much (or any) alone time. Our kids obviously wanted a lot of our attention. They had seen the rest of the family the previous few weeks, so now it was time for Mommy and Daddy. And, we were missing them, too, so we couldn't resist taking the time to talk, snuggle, listen, play games, watch them play games, etc. We also had family and friends coming in and out, including those who had been providing meals through mealtrain.com (we can never thank everyone enough for all of their support!).

I was just so prayerful that people would understand my need to lessen the updates. Plus, there wasn't as much to update. Paul still needed prayers, but the urgent needs were becoming less and less. Praise God! With that in mind, I knew there were so many others who were in need of urgent prayers. I wanted to keep everyone updated and have them share in our journey, but I didn't want to ask for more than we needed. We received the prayers we needed when they were urgently required. I was certain there were others needing that same urgent prayer support for other reasons. So, I was trying to find the balance between updating, sharing, and asking for prayers.

Something else I didn't add was that we were finally at the point to let my sister, Tammy, go back home. While this meant that things were improving, and we didn't need the constant support at the house with the kids; it also meant that the stability in the house would be changing. Tammy had stopped her life for over four weeks to be the stable rock in our home. We were so very thankful for all that she had done for us, and we would all miss her dearly.

Sunday, March 15 – Monday, March 16, 2015

Here is a perfect example of what I was just mentioning about finding time and balance. I didn't even send an update on Sunday. It was Monday morning before I sent this update:

> **March 15th-16th Reports:**
> UPDATE: Yesterday was a good & busy day!
>
> Paul shaved-which is great because I shaved him last time. Let's just say I will not be pursuing that as my next career.

> Paulie had baseball practice at 1:30, so the four of us went there. Paul and I were getting some steps in while Noah was trying to chase us. It was lots of fun. And, it was fun to watch Paulie practice!
>
> When we got home, Paul and I were able to take a walk around the subdivision and both get our 10,000 steps for the day! Praise God for healing Paul!
>
> Today is another day of dialysis. Since this is outpatient, I am not sure what news I will hear. If I get more info, I will post.
>
> One last note - What we were not expecting is the significant weight loss. Paul went into the hospital at 235lbs. Yesterday, he was down to 214lbs. We will talk with the dietitian as he needs to increase his calorie count while keeping the other chemicals/minerals below the threshold.
>
> Our prayer today is that Paul's kidneys kick in by Spring Break. While we know our plans for Great Wolf Lodge are changed, we would love to visit family or go somewhere that week. We are praying Paul will be done with dialysis by then. While the kidneys do not have a timeline, we are asking God for this additional miracle!
>
> Thank you all! Much love!

There was a lot of information in this update. First, Paul finally shaved. When he was in the ICU, the nurses did their best to shave him. When he transitioned to the medical unit, I tried to shave him once – which was *not* a huge success. Seriously, the hair on a man's face is significantly different than the hair on a woman's legs. Let's just say – it was not a clean shave. When he was done shaving himself, he looked so very handsome. He was starting to look more and more like he looked prior to this entire ordeal.

That afternoon, Paulie had baseball practice. He had made the travel team and practices had started during the time Paul was in the hospital. The coach was also a neighbor, so he had been picking Paulie up and bringing him home from practice. We felt it was time for us to take him ourselves.

When we arrived, the few who knew about Paul's journey were quick to come up and talk with us. They were so thankful to see Paul and hear of his progress. There were also some who kept their distance. Having been in their shoes, I know that they just didn't know what to say. They were happy to see Paul walking around, and didn't want him to have to repeat the story again and again. They would motion to us or give us a head nod. When our eyes met, we could see their eyes well up in tears. They didn't have the words, but their eyes said it all. And, truly, that was plenty.

After practice started, we went upstairs to walk the track. I was impressed by Paul's ability to get around the track. Once he started, he showed little signs of stopping! He was determined to exceed 10,000 steps on Sunday.

When practice was over, we both had about 2,000 steps remaining to exceed 10,000 steps. When we got home, Paul's parents watched the kids, and we took our first walk around the neighborhood. Each time we did something new, I stopped for a moment to recognize just how important that new experience was. The last time Paul was home, it was snowing and we would not have walked around the neighborhood. Today, it was chilly, but comfortable. We walked around the neighborhood together and talked. Even after we exceeded 10,000 steps, we continued walking for some time. It felt so normal, and so new at the same time. We had so very much to be thankful for!

After all of that activity, Paul and I were both pretty wiped. We knew Monday would be another long day – including a 4-hour dialysis run. We kissed each other goodnight, and I again asked Paul to "marry me". I had been asking him this each night since we discussed it in the hospital, and he, in turn, would ask me each morning. While it might seem silly, to us, it was important. We wanted to remind ourselves – every morning and every night – just how much we mean to each other. God had saved Paul, He had kept us together as a family, and we didn't want to minimize how important that was.

Thankfully, Paul agreed to marry me and we drifted off to sleep.

Monday, March 16, 2015

Paul had a really great night of sleep – probably the best sleep in over a month! He woke up refreshed and ready to take on another day of dialysis. One of my concerns was his rapid weight loss. I guess I just didn't realize how much his muscles would have atrophied during his time in the hospital. But, they did, and it was showing in his weight. He was down at least 21lbs. And, I was concerned about what I was feeding him. *Was I giving him enough calories? Was I starving him? Was I doing damage to his kidneys?*

When we arrived at the dialysis center, I spoke with the dietitian about Paul's diet and my concerns about his weight. She calmed me down, and helped me to realize just how much weight Paul had lost through the breakdown of his muscles. She also shared that this was not likely his lowest weight, but gave me better options for meals to help increase his calorie intake. I was so very thankful for this information – I felt better equipped to help him moving forward.

I was also praying for Paul's kidneys to heal before Spring Break. We had previously scheduled a trip to the Great Wolf Lodge. We were all very excited to go, but when Paul was in the hospital, I cancelled the trip. While I was always focused on Paul waking up and coming home, I just felt it would be too much, too soon. Since our Spring Break wouldn't include that trip, I was at least hoping we would be able to visit our family or do something fun during that week. Our kids had been through so much; I wanted to give them something to look forward to doing.

Paul had another good dialysis session, and we had another good day. We were able to see Paulie before he left for school, and see the kids when Paul got home from dialysis. We, then, were able to get Paulie off of the bus, and hear about his amazing day at school. We spent time with our family still at the house and more neighbors and friends who stopped by. And, after yet another full day, we settled into bed.

We had left the routine of the hospital and were finding our new routine back at home. While things needed to change due to the increase in doctor's visits and dialysis, there were still so many familiar things that were kept in our routine. We were all so very thankful for the old routine – mixed in with these new needs.

Chapter 28: God is Good – ALWAYS!

Tuesday, March 17, 2015

One thing I haven't mentioned was that Paul wanted to sleep on my side of the bed. His side wasn't as comfortable, so I offered to switch. I thought this offer was a one to two night agreement. Little did I know that, five nights later, we would still be sleeping on opposite sides. And, his side was definitely less comfortable than mine. Regardless, I would do anything to make his sleep more comfortable. I would give him the entire bed and sleep on a bed of stones if that would help him get a restful sleep.

"I sure hope, when he reads this, he doesn't take me up on that offer!"

Here was my morning report:

> **March 17th - Morning Report:**
> UPDATE: Paul had another great night of sleep last night! I guess it's official - I have lost my side of the bed ☺.
>
> What we are learning is that outpatient dialysis is very different that inpatient dialysis. Paul will not be getting labs as often as he did in the hospital. And, it takes 48 hours to get the results. So, while I was hoping to know Paul's numbers when I picked him up on Monday afternoon, I will likely not see them until I pick him up on Wednesday. I am praying for patience with this change, as I know they know what they are doing - and Paul is doing GREAT! There is something comforting about knowing the numbers immediately (not that I can control any of it, I just like knowing the information).

> After dialysis yesterday, I dropped Paul off at home with his mom & the kids and I went to an HBA meeting. It was so wonderful seeing these amazing women! I was able to get many hugs and lots of support. It was a true blessing to be there!
>
> And, while I was gone, Paul took another walk around the subdivision. While he didn't get to 10,000 steps, he was able to get some…even after a 4-hour dialysis run - WooHoo!
>
> We are deciding what to do with this glorious day! One thing is for sure - our itty bittys need a BATH! So, we will do that first and get the family dressed in green.
>
> Happy St. Patrick's Day to All!!! Much Love!

When Paul was discharged from the hospital, I knew there would be significant change. What I didn't realize was just how much change. I was learning to take on new roles in our family, and specifically for Paul – as his pharmacist and dietitian. What I wasn't anticipating is the difference in the amount of information I would have.

At the hospital, Paul had at least one set of labs each day. Before 8:00am, we had the results of those labs that then dictated the remainder of the day. On Monday, I learned that the outpatient facility usually runs labs once per month on most patients. These are usually patients with chronic kidney disease, so they don't require immediate lab results. For them, drawing labs once per week for Paul was a significant increase compared to their usual patients. For us, it was a significant decrease compared to the daily (or sometimes twice daily) lab draws. I knew I had to trust God. He would show us if something was going wrong and help us make the right decisions. He had gotten Paul this far; I needed to trust Him. I am not saying this was easy, but I knew it was what I needed to do.

Monday afternoon, with family still helping at the house, I did take the opportunity to go to my Healthcare Businesswomen's Association (HBA) meeting. These women were there every step of this journey. I knew they wanted to hear the updates, and I needed the hugs and support. It was great seeing all of them, and sharing our overwhelming gratitude for all they had done to help us. While it was a very tearful meeting, it was so needed.

With Monday being such a full day for all of us, we had a great rest on Monday night. We woke up on Tuesday and were ready to take on the day. God had given us a beautiful morning and we wanted to make the most of it. But, first, we needed to get the kids clean. Such a simple thing to do, but it had been weeks since Paul and I helped the kids take a bath. We were both so very grateful that God had seen us to this stage in the journey, and that we were able to help the kids. We felt very blessed and grateful.

So, the kids were clean and Paul took this selfie in his St. Patrick's Day green (I really should have taken more of the pictures):

We had a great day together as a family. That night, before I went to sleep, I felt called to write an additional post. Paul and I had a very specific conversation about the "what ifs". What I didn't quite realize was just how often God had moved my thoughts from the "what ifs" to the present progress. While I can't say I didn't think of alternate scenarios, God didn't let me dwell there.

We also spent time discussing how great God is and was during this entire journey. And, while I wasn't sure how Paul would react, I said that God would have been just as great regardless of Paul's outcome. I was so thankful that Paul agreed. While we were so thankful for all God had done, He would have still been just as amazing if the outcome were different. Here was that post:

March 17th – God is Good – Always!

God is good - Always! And, when I say always, I mean always. God's greatness is not wrapped up in any outcome / any result. God's greatness is beyond measure.

Psalm 18:30 (CEB):
God! His way is perfect; the Lord's word is tried and true. He is a shield for all who take refuge in him.

Why am I writing about this? And, why now?

Remember the night I broke down? I came home and wrapped my arms around my sister and cried. As we stood there, I said -

"I know God has a plan. But, what if His plan is not healing Paul? What if Paul doesn't wake up? I trust God. I believe in Him and know He will make beauty out of any crisis. Can we please pray that whatever God's plan is today, that He makes His plan a full recovery for Paul?"

So, we prayed. We prayed for God's plan to be Paul's full recovery. We prayed that God would provide all of us with His "peace beyond understanding." And, we continued praying boldly. Boldly for healing. Boldly for God's plan to be complete recovery. Boldly for peace...

***Philippians 4:6-7 (GNB):**
Don't worry about anything, but in all your prayers ask God for what you need, always asking him with a thankful heart. And God's peace, which is far beyond human understanding, will keep your hearts and minds safe in union with Christ Jesus.*

As Paul and I were heading to dialysis yesterday, we talked about this. We discussed God's greatness - and how that wouldn't change even if Paul didn't "wake up." How we prayed boldly for God's plan to be for Paul's complete recovery, but that was never guaranteed. Regardless - God is now and always will be faithful, all-knowing, all-powerful and ever-loving

It probably seems easy for me to share this now considering we have come out of the darkest hours of this journey. Please know I wanted to share this earlier, but there was a part of me that was fearful to write this down. I know that may seem quite silly (and I feel silly writing it), but there was part of me that didn't want to put that down as I felt it would have been me giving up on Him. Giving into my fears of what might come and focusing on a negative outcome. So, while I didn't write it, I was so very thankful for my sister to be able to talk about it.

I am also very thankful that God helped me keep my eyes and vision on Paul's complete healing. Whenever my mind would shift to something other than that, I felt a gentle nudge away from those thoughts. During one of our recent conversations,

Paul asked where I would have buried him. (I hope you never have to have that conversation with your loved ones!!). I was able to share - my mind NEVER went there. When I would think of any part of my life without Paul, God would gently bring me back to full healing. He would show me walking out of the hospital with Paul, hand-in-hand, coming home to our children.

I have a few friends in the middle of deep crises right now. Their outcomes are definitely not positive. We have been praying for God's peace beyond understanding to help them through these difficult times. I also received the best advice from a friend a few years ago that fits during times like these.

Cry out to God. Tell Him how you feel. Yell about the situation. God can handle your anger. God knows your pain.
He is crying with you and for you.

Psalm 23:4 (NLT):
Even when I walk through the darkest valley, I will not be afraid, for you are close beside me. Your rod and your staff protect and comfort me.

While I cannot say that I didn't ever fear, I did always know that God would see us through that valley - regardless of the outcome.

Father,

We are forever grateful for Your amazing blessings and miracles in healing Paul. You have healed his mind, his heart, his lungs, his liver, and his skin. You have already started the healing of his kidneys. You woke him up with a prayerful and thankful heart - seeking a closer relationship with You.

> *That said, Your greatness is not dependent on that outcome. You are ALWAYS great! You are ALWAYS faithful. You will help each of us come through the darkest valleys and see something beautiful come out of the chaos. And, You are ALWAYS with us!*
>
> *Father, please stay close to those who are in the middle of those valleys. Please hold them in Your Arms and help them to feel Your Presence. Please help them to know Your peace beyond understanding.*
>
> *In Jesus' Name,*
> *Amen!*

This was such an important discussion with Paul. I truly didn't know how he would react to the statement – *God is good regardless of outcome*. Especially after all that Paul had just been through (and was still going through), I didn't want him to think I was minimizing his importance to me. Instead, I was maximizing God's importance to me, to him, to all of us. And, Paul agreed. Regardless of the outcome, Paul would want our kids to know that God was and is always good, always faithful, ever-living, and ever-loving.

After the conversation, I knew I wanted to share that post. There was a part of me that wished I had shared it sooner, but I couldn't change that. What I did realize was part of why I didn't share it sooner. Yes, I said that I didn't want it to seem like I had given up, and that was very true. I didn't want others reading it to think that my head and heart were on anything other than complete recovery. The other thing – the sillier thing – was that I didn't want to "taunt" God. I know that sounds a bit crazy. But, that was how I felt. In the middle of it, I didn't want to publicly write, *"God is good regardless of outcome"* for the fear that God would say, *"Ok, prove it."* I see just how irrational that thinking was. But, it was how I felt at the time.

So, sharing this wasn't easy. I didn't quite know how people would react to it. Plus, as I mentioned, we had some friends going through some very difficult trials. Some had potential positive outcomes and others seemed dire. I thought a lot about delaying this post. I didn't want people to think I was minimizing their experience. But, I felt God nudge me to write it. This was the perfect time. No matter how bad the situation might appear, nothing was ever impossible for God. That doesn't mean that everything would always have a positive outcome. It just meant that anything was possible, and God was and is worth believing in. And, when the outcomes aren't what we had hoped, desired, dreamed and prayed about, God would make beauty out of that, too. It may take time, but God has and always will see us through.

Chapter 29: Coming Full Circle

Wednesday, March 18, 2015

It was Wednesday morning, so that meant it was dialysis day. It also meant it was numbers day. Since we hadn't gotten numbers from the outpatient center yet, I wasn't certain how open they would be about sharing the report. I was hopeful it would be an easy process, but prepared a conversation on the importance of my receiving the labs in case they were less willing. To my pleasant surprise, they were more than willing to share the report. They had one printed and ready for me when we got there. Praise God!

Here was the daily update:

> **March 18th - Full Day Report:**
>
> UPDATE: Today was a very full day!
>
> Paul was called in early for dialysis today. We were somewhat looking forward to dialysis today - well, at least getting Paul's numbers. And - they are looking better! Hallelujah!
>
> Paul's creatinine was still 8.5, but considering that was before dialysis on Monday, that is a good number. We were thinking it might be up near 12 as that was what it was on Friday.
>
> All of his other numbers are looking much better. Sodium, Calcium, Potassium & Phosphorus were all within normal range. That was good news for me as that means the diet I am feeding him is working and his kidneys are keeping the numbers in a good range. Praise God!
>
> Paul is continuing to lose weight. He is down to 211lbs - with shoes on. The good news is the dietitian is willing to let Paul

> have some donuts!! He is looking forward to adding a few pounds back with a trip to Dunkin Donuts!
>
> We are praying for another good day tomorrow. I am planning on spending the day at Butler (last month, I was at Butler when I received the call to come home and all of this ordeal started).
>
> Thank you all for your prayers & support! We cannot tell you how much we truly appreciate it! We are forever grateful!

Hallelujah! This was the first set of kidney labs that were showing signs of the filter kicking back it. We were over-the-moon when we saw these numbers. While they were still **way too high** (normal is 0.6 – 1.3), the 8.5 was much better than the 12 we were expecting.

Paul was also still losing weight. This was due in part to the pulling of fluid from dialysis and in part from my fear of feeding him. He was probably getting about ~1500 calories per day. They wanted me to get him up to at least 2000 calories per day, but I was struggling to get there. I would look at every label and measure out what Paul could have per meal and in the overall day. The dietitian was great helping me with different options for Paul.

The next day was going to be a full one. I was planning to be at an all-day women's leadership meeting at Butler. This was the same meeting I was at the month prior when this journey started. Paul wanted me to go, and I knew it would be good for me to have some time away, too. Plus, we still had family at our house who were willing to help, so I agreed to go. I spent much of Wednesday evening planning Paul's day on Thursday without me. I knew they could have handled it without any direction from me, and I was so thankful they allowed me to provide them the information. They could have told me – *"We've got this. Don't worry. Go and have fun."* But, I would have been worried the entire time. Their willingness to let me plan the day helped me know that everything was going to be okay…even if they didn't do a thing I recommended.

Thursday, March 19 – Friday, March 20, 2015

When I woke up on Thursday, I was questioning my decision to go to the meeting. While I knew it would be good for me to spend some "me" time, I wasn't sure I should be gone for a full day. Our family had done so very much for us these past four weeks. I didn't feel it was fair to them. But, they also thought I should go. Soon, they would need to return to their lives and I would have fewer opportunities to do things on my own. So, I agreed and off to Butler I went.

What I didn't anticipate was just how hard that drive down to Butler would be. I could not stop crying. Four weeks prior, I had been at this meeting when I received the text from Paul to come home. That night, we didn't know if he would make it the next minute – now, I was heading back to campus the next month. I was so very thankful we had gotten here in such a short amount of time, and I was also so very aware of just how different our lives were now.

When I walked into the meeting room, there were lots of hugs and tears. I shared part of our journey with the women as we greeted each other. They had all been following the posts, so they knew how things were with Paul. They were also concerned with how I was doing. I hadn't given much information on how I was, and they all wanted to be there for me as I processed this journey. They also wanted to give me something to wrap up in, to always know they were thinking of us – thinking of me.

This blanket is filled with very uplifting sayings and quotes. The women had been sending these to each other and I captured them prior to our February meeting. For our March meeting, they put them on this blanket. We are truly blessed to have such amazing people in our lives!

As I spent the rest of the day with these amazing women, Paul spent the day with his mom and the kids. They were able to run a few errands and get out of the house to somewhere other than dialysis. This was important for Paul, too.

Here was the update for both Thursday and Friday:

> **March 19th-20th - Update:**
> Paul had a great day off dialysis! He was able to spend a good day with his mom and the kids. He feels so much better on his non-dialysis days.
>
> He was able to run a few errands with his mom and the itty bittys. While he hasn't driven yet, just getting out of the house to go somewhere outside of dialysis is always good for him.

I spent the day with my amazing AWL friends! So thankful for all of them!

I was able to listen to the end of the Butler game - that was too close for comfort! We are looking forward to being a house divided tomorrow night when Butler plays ND. Hoping for a great game and a Butler Bulldogs win! Go DAWGS!!!

We then went to Paulie's baseball practice. It was the first one outside, so Paul and I were able to walk around the fields while Paulie was practicing. We stopped to watch him play quite a bit. He is definitely getting better and having a blast!

Paul did step on the scale yesterday morning and was at an all-time low (well at least in our marriage) - 207! It looks like he's got that weight loss challenge in the bag!

Today, they are challenging his kidneys to see if they can remove some additional fluid. While Paul is at his lowest weight, that doesn't mean there isn't still some extra fluid that needs to be removed. I am leaving to pick him up soon, so we will see how that went.

We are looking forward to a great evening of basketball and family time! Thank you all for continuing your prayers & support. We are ever so grateful for you!

We are continuing our prayers for:
- Complete healing of kidneys
- Patience in the process

As Paul and I talk about this journey, we realize this story is truly a story of the Power of God, His Grace and His Glory! We are blessed to be able to share His story through our experiences to show He is a Living & Loving God! And we are thankful to be "living" proof of His Great Grace!

> One new song to share - Hawk Nelson - Drops in the Ocean
> https://www.youtube.com/watch?v=bZHI3wFGffg
>
> Been listening to this song on repeat!

On my way home from Butler, I was able to listen to their game. It was a close win, but it was a win. That meant an ND vs. Butler matchup. That would definitely be a house divided, as Paul (and his entire family) are die-hard ND fans. I would put myself in that camp, too, except when they play Butler. So, it was going to be a fun evening on Saturday.

Thursday evening, we were able to get outside a bit to watch Paulie's baseball practice. He was having so much fun, and he was learning a ton about the game of baseball. We were so grateful to be there, to watch him, to be together. How different life would have been...

On Friday, I drove Paul to dialysis and they told us they were going to challenge his kidneys. Even though Paul weighed much less than he did when he entered the hospital, they explained that didn't mean that Paul wasn't still carrying extra fluid around his body. So, they would pull more fluid to see how Paul's body responded. Based on that, they would determine if he was finally at his "dry weight". I wasn't quite sure what that weight would be, as Paul already looked so thin. But, I knew that he lost a lot of muscle mass in the hospital and muscle weighs more than fat. Plus, I felt very confident the doctors, nurses and staff knew what they were doing. They would take care of Paul, and I needed to trust that.

When I picked Paul up, he had done amazingly well. They were able to pull more fluid from him, and his body didn't react. So, we weren't at his final "dry weight", but they would be working on getting him there.

We drove home and talked about just how grateful we were for all the miracles God had provided and all of the blessings in our lives. We were so thankful for so many who lifted us up in prayer and provided other help and support. While we were not at the end of this journey, we had come so far in such a short amount of time. We praised God for all of His work, and for surrounding us with such great family and friends.

We were also excited for our first full weekend at home without dialysis. We had family in town, so we were hoping that we would have a weekend that was closer to a "normal" weekend – prior to Paul getting sick. While we weren't exactly sure what the weekend would hold, we were both very excited about the possibilities.

Chapter 30: Our "New" Normal

Saturday, March 21, 2015

Paul had a hard time falling asleep and staying asleep Friday night. When he would get excited about something happening the next day, he would often react this way – little to no sleep. And, Friday night was no different. While Paul was excited about the ND vs. Butler basketball game, he was even more excited about another game. Remember when I shared that Paul would play basketball several times per week? One of his favorites was Saturday morning at 6:00am. It was a great way to start his day – with exercise and time with the guys.

A friend from that group was moving to South Bend, so this would be his last Saturday morning game, and Paul wanted to be there to say good-bye. Even though Paul was not going to be able to play, he would be there to say hello and good-bye.

He was also very excited and nervous about driving himself for the first time. He felt confident he could drive, but hadn't done it yet. This was a great test of his ability to be fully independent. Plus, he had asked Paulie to go with him; so while he would be driving, he wouldn't be alone. Paulie would be there to help…well, at least as much as a 7-year-old can help.

Here was the update:

> **March 21st Report:**
> UPDATE: Paul didn't sleep that well last night. I think it was because he was excited about his morning. He took Paulie to his Saturday morning (6:00am) basketball game. While Paul is not in any shape to play, he wanted to go to say goodbye to a friend who is moving to South Bend.

This was a big deal for a few reasons:

1-this is the first time Paul drove. He has felt confident in his ability to drive - this was the first time he actually did it. He said he felt good which is great news!!
2-He also got a sense of just how many people have been praying for him. He was amazed both by the number of people and by how they found out. I still don't think either of us truly have a clue as to just how many people have been following us and praying with us through this journey. We are forever grateful!

The rest of the day should be a good one for us. Paul's parents are here with us. We are looking forward to family time, basketball & church. Today is the feast day for St. Benedict - the Patron Saint of kidney disease.

We were also honored to be asked to participate in the Holy Thursday services. They have asked us to present the Oil of the Sick. We are hoping Paul feels good enough to do that himself. If not, I will step in on his behalf.

Our prayers continue to be for kidneys and for patience. And, I am sure there will be many conflicting prayers being said tonight during the Butler v ND game. I hope it's a great game with a Butler victory!

Paul did it! He drove and felt comfortable doing it. He was able to get himself to the court and back. He also did some laps with Paulie while he was there. He wasn't able to play basketball, but at least he was able to get some exercising in.

This experience also gave Paul a greater understanding of just how many people were praying for him. There were some who had asked to be my friend on Facebook or followed the blog. He knew the updates were there, but it surprised him how many were reading them. Then, he talked with a few people who had heard from others in the community. He didn't know how they knew, and had a hard time understanding why they would have been sharing information about him. See, Paul still didn't quite get just how sick he had gotten, and just how sick he still was. And, Paul does not like attention. So, in his mind, he was getting better. No need to talk about him – what was there to talk about? This experience gave him greater insights into just how many people cared and were praying for him.

We had another big day planned. We attended Saturday evening mass. This was the first time Paul was back in church. We were so very thankful for everyone at church who lifted Paul and our family up in prayer throughout this journey, and for both Father and Deacon visiting us at the hospital so very often during Paul's twenty-two days there. Plus, it was the Feast Day of St. Benedict – the Patron Saint of kidney disease. There couldn't be a more perfect day for Paul's first day back at mass. And, we could use the extra prayer support for Paul's kidneys.

I also mentioned that we had been asked to carry the "Oil of the Sick" at Holy Thursday mass. This was the very oil that Paul was anointed with, twice, while he was "sleeping". What an honor it was to be asked! We were so thankful for the opportunity and quickly accepted. We hoped Paul would feel up to the task. While he isn't a big fan of speaking in public, or being the center of attention, we both agreed this would be a great opportunity. If Paul would not have been able, I would be the back up, but we prayed for Paul's strength and ability to do this.

After mass, we settled in for the ND vs. Butler basketball game. While Paul and I were firmly in our camps, Paulie was split. He brought down both jerseys and switched them a few times during the game. Even though ND pulled off the win, Butler played a great game. Always proud to be a Bulldog!

Sunday, March 22 – Sunday, March 29, 2015

This was our 2nd full week at home, and we were getting used to our new normal. On Sunday evening, Paul's mom went back home with his dad. It wasn't easy for them to leave, but it was time. They had gotten us through the toughest part of the journey; it was time for them to get back to their lives. We were planning to see them the next weekend to celebrate Easter, so it wouldn't be long before we were together again. But, that wasn't it. It was the acknowledgement of all that had happened. It was the awareness that, several weeks ago, we didn't know that this day would come. And, now it was here. No words, lots of tears and hugs. Praise You, Lord, for bringing us through this!

While we were sad to see Paul's parents go, we were also thankful to have additional help for one more week. Our dear friend (our former neighbor) took the week off of work to come down and help us for the week. We are so truly blessed!

Paul had dialysis Monday, Wednesday and Friday. His lab report on Wednesday again showed marked improvement. His creatinine was down to 4.9 – Praise God! Again, we still had a ways to go, but the continued improvement was a lot to be thankful for.

Paul was still losing weight. They found his "dry weight" at 202lbs. This was quite different for me as Paul's lowest weight in our relationship had been ~220lbs. He spent most of our years together in the 240s (up to 260 and down to 230). Now, he was 202lbs, and he still hadn't gained his strength yet. We weren't sure what Paul's new normal would be, and we had time before we needed to worry about that.

Paul was happy to learn he had been cleared to start physical therapy. He was worried about the dialysis port still being in and his ability to work on his strength. But, the doctor felt confident, so Paul scheduled to meet with the PT the next week. He would have an assessment done to determine how many sessions would be needed. He was just happy to have someone help him and let him know what he could and couldn't do. Paul was determined to get stronger and feel better. I am so thankful for that determination. He could have woken up so very differently. Praising God for Paul's drive, determination and grateful heart!

Chapter 31: Holy Week – Deepening Our Relationship with Christ

Monday, March 30 – Sunday, April 5, 2015

Our Monday morning started like the previous two weeks except for one major difference – it was just the five of us. For nearly six weeks, we always had someone else at the house to help. Sometimes, we had a house full and other times it was just my sister, Paul's mom and/or my friend.

It was now just up to us. We needed to figure out how to get Paul to dialysis. Paulie was on Spring Break, so that made things easier. While we had a couple of options, Paul really wanted to drive himself to dialysis. This would not have been possible the first week. However, he was handling the procedures well and was much less drained than before. He felt strong enough to handle it, and I agreed he should try it. So, he drove himself to dialysis and I took care of the kids. And, as expected, Paul did great!

We also had Holy Thursday practice on Monday evening. Paul had been continuing to improve each day, so we felt strongly that he should be the one to take up the "Oil of the Sick". Paul had a few sentences to read, and didn't know if he needed to memorize them or if they would be available to read. So, he was practicing and trying to remember them, just in case.

When we got to the church, we learned they would have the reading available for him, which made Paul much more comfortable. Paul went through the practice and then we went out for a family dinner. It was our first dinner out with just us. We took extra time in our prayer before our meal to share just how thankful we were for how far we have come.

Here was my post from Monday:

> **March 30th Report:**
>
> UPDATE: Paul had a really good weekend (well, other than the ND loss to Kentucky). It was a nice weekend spending time with family!
>
> Paul got the call to come in early for dialysis today. While that is usually a good thing because Paul likes to go early, we don't have any one staying with us this week. So Paul drove himself to dialysis this morning. I am not so worried about the morning trip, but I am worried about him driving home after dialysis. I know others do this, it's just not something we have had to worry about because of our amazing family & friends! He will call me when it is over and, if he is tired, we will go & get him.
>
> We also have practice for Holy Thursday services tonight. Looking forward to going and to having Paul present the Oil of the Sick at mass on Thursday. What a true honor to be asked. We personally have seen the power of prayer!
>
> This Holy Week has an even deeper meaning to us this year. We have witnessed God work miracles in Paul!
>
> > *Ephesians 2:8-9(GNB):*
> > *For it is by God's grace that you have been saved through faith. It is not the result of your own efforts, but God's gift, so that no one can boast about it.*
>
> My prayer this Holy Week is both for the complete healing for Paul's kidneys and for all of us to continue to deepen our relationship with Christ. He died on the cross so that each & every one of us could have the opportunity to go to Heaven.

If you believe God saved Paul because He has great plans for him (like I do), it shouldn't be hard to believe that God also has great plans for you!

> ***Romans 10:9-13 (GNB):***
> *If you confess that Jesus is Lord and believe that God raised him from death, you will be saved. For it is by our faith that we are put right with God; it is by our confession that we are saved. The scripture says, "Whoever believes in him will not be disappointed." This includes everyone, because there is no difference between Jews and Gentiles; God is the same Lord of all and richly blesses all who call to him. As the scripture says, "Everyone who calls out to the Lord for help will be saved."*

__Note:__ As you may have read in the introduction of this book, I had wanted to write a book for some time. That said, I didn't quite know what the topic would be. It was during Holy Week when this became very clear to me. My book was to be about this story, God's story, God's miracle of healing Paul, God's work of lifting up a community to pray so deeply. As I thought about the importance of Holy Week, I realized how many years I had gone through Lent and Holy Week as more of a process. I would give something up, but wouldn't think about what that meant. I would go to church, usually only on Easter Sunday. A few years, we had gone through the Stations of the Cross, but still – I didn't get it. These were just things that I did. I didn't fully grasp the meaning, the importance, the relationship.

I had come to know God through Jesus in a very different way the previous eight years. That relationship was the reason

I was able to get through this journey to this point. God was there holding me up when I couldn't stand, moving my feet when I couldn't walk, and taking a breath when I couldn't breathe. He helped me to stay focused on Him at times when all else seemed lost. When the world said it was impossible, God showed me – showed all of us – with him, anything is possible. God provides miracles everyday – both big and small. This was just another one of His everyday miracles. And, I was honored to be able to share this story. But, there was more work to do, so the writing of the story would need to wait.

On Thursday, Paul was able to walk down the "Oil of the Sick" at Holy Thursday mass. While most in church that evening didn't know Paul's story, we knew. We were so thankful that Paul was able to participate in that mass, the mass that blesses the oil that was used on him.

Here is my best effort of a family selfie at Church. Now you see why Paul takes the pictures in our family.

Easter Sunday family photo... and yes, those are the same outfits. In our defense, we were at a different church.

On Friday, Paul went back for dialysis and then we drove up to Northwest Indiana to celebrate Easter with Paul's family. We would celebrate with my family the following weekend back in Indianapolis. It was a great break for Paul to get out of the house and spend time with his family, especially now that he was feeling stronger! Again, we had so very much to be thankful for!

Chapter 32: Hallelujah & Amen! Praise God for all of Paul's Progress!

Monday, April 6 – Monday, April 13, 2015

After a wonderful weekend with family celebrating Easter, we came back home and settled in for our 2nd week together with just the five of us. We would again need to find our new rhythm, as this week was different than the last.

When Paul was at the dialysis center, they drew the blood for labs and started his dialysis. They told him that, based on those lab results, he may not need to come in on Wednesday. They were pleased with the way his kidneys were improving and felt he was close to being done with dialysis. He would need to keep the port in for a while longer, just in case he needed to have another dialysis run. So, whenever they stopped, he would need to still come in for weekly labs, but they thought the dialysis would soon be done.

As you can imagine, Paul was ecstatic! This would be his fourth week on outpatient dialysis. And, while the people were nice and the process had gotten much easier, he was ready to be done *as soon as possible*. So, we prayed that God would heal Paul's kidneys enough to let this be the last dialysis session.

Here was my post from Tuesday afternoon:

> **April 7th Report – Off Dialysis!:**
> We just received the call from the dialysis center and Paul's labs have improved enough to stop dialysis! Praise God!
>
> He will need to get his labs taken the next two Mondays and see the kidney doctor on 4/24. Until then, he will remain on

> the renal diet and continue with the doctor orders - but HE IS OFF DIALYSIS!
>
> Quick set of numbers:
> - Creatinine - down to 2.6
> - Diet Labs - all still high side of normal (surprising due to the Easter meal - Yum!)
> - White Blood Cells - back up in the normal range
>
> We cannot thank everyone enough for your prayers, love & support!! When this all started, no one knew what the outcome would be:
> - Would Paul wake up?
> - If so, would there be permanent damage?
> - And, how long would it take to get back to a "new normal"?
> - How would this impact our kids?
> - What would life be like?
> - And, so many more questions...
>
> What is so amazing about God is that He kept our focus on the positives, the improvements, the next blessing. He didn't allow us to focus on the negatives. He didn't give us time for that - Praise Him!
>
> We will post updates as we learn more. In the meantime, thank you, thank you, thank you! You have all prayed and seen God, our living-God, provide miracles in the healing of Paul!

Tears are streaming down my face as I re-read the post from that day. Amen! Amen! Hallelujah! Amen! We love a truly amazing God! What an answer to a very specific prayer – Paul would be off dialysis. Praise Him!

We took time to celebrate that significant milestone. While that didn't mean Paul was forever done with dialysis, it did mean that he was off of it for a little while. Paul's kidneys were improving, as was his strength. Just thinking about how much had improved the previous 6 ½ weeks was amazing! We had so very much to be thankful for!

Monday, April 13 – Tuesday, April 14, 2015

We prepared ourselves for another full week. Paul had his labs drawn on Monday and we patiently (or not so patiently) waited for the news. On Tuesday, we received the lab results and I posted this:

> **April 14th Update – Port is Coming Out!:**
> UPDATE: Praise the Lord! They will be removing Paul's dialysis port as soon as we can get it scheduled!
>
> Paul had his labs drawn yesterday - here are some quick numbers:
>
> Creatinine - down to 2.4 from 2.6 with only one day of dialysis which was last week Monday
>
> GFR is up to 33 which is still really low, but it was 8 at the hospital.
>
> All other diet numbers were looking good - still high side of normal, but that means his kidneys have to be working better because he has been pressing the boundaries of his diet!
>
> We received the information from the doctor's office via e-mail with a note that the doctor wants to schedule a time to pull the port soon! Hallelujah! We sent them some dates and will hopefully get that scheduled within the next week.
>
> Strength - Paul is continuing his PT and is getting stronger each day. And, he is currently kicking my butt in steps (I think that says more about my laziness than his activity...well, maybe a little bit of both). Paul was also excited to talk with his PT today about getting back onto the golf course. He ended his PT session today with working on the golf swing motion :).

> We truly want to thank everyone for all of your prayers & support for Paul and our family! It hasn't been an easy few months, but God is always good and you have all been amazing! We are truly blessed to have such great family & friends!
>
> Amen! Amen! Hallelujah & Amen!!!

Praise God! Not only was Paul off dialysis, but now he was getting the port removed! His lab values were improving with each draw, and Paul was getting stronger. He was even back swinging a golf club at PT. While he wished he was back on the basketball court, he was at least able to get in more steps and increase his strength and activity. Amen!

Chapter 33: What about Me? Where is God Guiding My Next Step?

Wednesday, April 15 – Sunday, April 19, 2015

With every improvement Paul was experiencing, people would ask more and more about me. How was I feeling? What did I need? What would be next for me? So, I wrote this:

> **April 15th – What's Next for Me?:**
>
> Thank you all so very much for your prayers & support for Paul. He is getting better each day, and we praise God for the miracles He has provided. We just learned that Paul's dialysis port will be removed this Friday - Hallelujah!!!
>
> I also appreciate the prayers & concern regarding what's next for me. With everything going on with Paul, I haven't taken much time to think it through. I know I have had the time, but I haven't taken the time. I've been avoiding it.
>
> Now that Paul is getting better, I need to take the time to think about my future - and that is truly frightening!
>
> For 16+ years, all I have known is Pfizer. I have had eight different positions in that time, and have had the opportunity to do really great work with amazing people. My last two positions were roles that were "pinnacle roles" for me - ones that I thought I might be doing near the end of my career - not in the middle of it.
>
> So…now what?
> - Do I stay at Pfizer?
> - Do I work somewhere else in healthcare?
> - Do I work somewhere else in another industry?
> - Do I work for a big company, small company?

- Do I start my own company?
- Do I write a book about all of this?

The irony is, I recently moderated a program on "Making the Most of Your Development Plan." Not only did I moderate this program, I co-created the entire program series. Now, here I sit, needing to put together my very own development plan. I need to take the time to identify where I want to go next. More importantly, what are God's plans for my next steps?

I was thinking about a post I wrote on January 30th titled "2015 - The Year of Growth". I wrote this while at a Christian Women's retreat called - the Soul Spa Sisterhood (the next one is coming up in May!). The point of this post was my desire to spend this year focusing my eyes on where God wants me to be. Where is He guiding my life? While I don't think God made all of this happen, I do fully believe He will use all of this to grow & strengthen us in preparation for His great plan. And, His plan is greater than I could ever imagine!!

> ***Ephesians 3:20 (GNB):***
> *To him who by means of his power working in us is able to do so much more than we can ever ask for, or even think of*
>
> ***Jeremiah 29:11 (GNB):***
> *I alone know the plans I have for you, plans to bring you prosperity and not disaster, plans to bring about the future you hope for*

So, I will take these next few weeks to pray, to seek God's guidance and make some decisions. I am truly thankful that I have the time to do this.

> I also offered to continue to work at Pfizer the next eight weeks to help move the projects we were planning for 2015 forward. While I don't have to do it, I want to set the projects up for success as I truly believe in the work we were doing.
>
> As my next step becomes clearer, I will definitely share. Until then, thank you all so very much for your prayers & support!!! XOXOX

Even though I didn't have many answers, I was at least very aware of my options. I even gently floated the idea of writing a book. I didn't want to publicly say, *"I am writing a book"*...at least not yet. If I didn't get it done, I didn't want to disappoint anyone. So, I added it in as an option, and I received lots of comments from our friends and family encouraging me to write the book. It is amazing how God continued to give me what I needed, when I needed it. I was just so thankful that my eyes, ears and heart were open to receiving it.

Our week was full of activity, and Friday, Paul had the port removed. It was a much easier procedure than either of us had imagined. We were home in time to get Paulie off of the bus and prepare for a fun-filled weekend. We had gotten used to having family and friends in town for the weekends, and this weekend would be no different. We felt truly blessed to have all of the love and support!

Monday, April 20 – Thursday, April 24, 2015

After a great weekend with the family, we again settled into another week of just the five of us. We had gotten used to our new roles. For the past two years, I had traveled a great deal, so the daily routine had been fully handled by Paul. When I was home, I would try to jump in and help, but it usually was less than helpful.

The first few weeks Paul was home, he wasn't able to participate in his old routine. My sister had a routine that was working when we were all at the hospital. When we came home, Paul's mom and I carried out that routine after my sister left. Then, I continued it as Paul was healing. Now, he was feeling better and wanting to be more help around the house and with the kids. While he couldn't do it all like he did before, I was grateful he was able to help.

I am still so very impressed by his ability to be a stay at home dad! He had taken on that role as soon as Paulie was born and has done it ever since. He is great at it! He has everything under control. While I always knew it was a lot and was very thankful for all Paul did, having to do the role myself gave me an even greater appreciation for ALL he did!

Monday morning, Paul had his labs drawn, and we received the update on Wednesday. Here was my post:

April 22nd Update:

UPDATE: We have been patiently (or not so patiently) awaiting the results from Paul's lab draw on Monday and praying for more positive improvements in his labs. Praising God for the results we just received!!!

Creatinine - down to 2.19 from 2.4 last week! Hallelujah! The normal range is 0.6-1.3, so he still has a little way to go. That said, this is significant improvement from the 12 & 13 we were seeing at the hospital!!!

BUN - This is also moving in the right direction. It was 33 this week, down from 36 the last two weeks. Normal again is 8-26. We are definitely getting there!

GFR - His GFR is 36, up from 33 last week. The goal here would be above 60, but he was in the single digits in the hospital.

Diet numbers - all still in the normal range. And when I say that Paul has been stretching the limits of the renal diet, that is definitely an understatement. Praise God!!!

Physical Strength - He is in Physical Therapy twice each week and is walking other days. He even made it to basketball on Monday night! While his jumper isn't what it used to be, he will get that back. And, he is working on his golf swing to be in shape for the Berger Open. Watch out boys!

Weight - I am not sure where he is looking to land on his weight. He was 255 in January when he started a diet challenge with his friends. He was around 235 when he went into the hospital. Today, he is 202 - a much healthier 202. Amen!!!

Me - I thought I would just add this in here, because it seems to fit. I have been praying about my next steps - what God's plan is for my journey. What I continue to receive is that I am supposed to write this story - God's story. So, I decided to write a book. I am not sure what God has planned for that book - maybe it's just for us or maybe it's meant for more. I'm not going to worry about any of that right now. Right now, I just want to focus on writing this story. It is truly hard to believe it hasn't even been 9 weeks!

Please know how much we truly love you all and are so very grateful for each & every one of you! Your prayers, love & support helped us to stay strong throughout this journey.

Heavenly Father,

We praise Your Glorious Name for ALL the miracles You provided in the healing of Paul. You made sure all the right decisions were made so that we could prove You are the ultimate healer! Paul is living proof that You continue to provide miracles on Earth!

> *Please know how much we love You, we thank You, we praise You!*
>
> *In Jesus' Name - AMEN!*

Praise God! Paul's kidneys were continuing to show signs of healing. Paul was getting stronger every day and his weight was down and stable. We were so very close to complete healing. Nine weeks prior, none of this seemed possible. Now, here we were. God is amazing!

I also finally decided to add my plans for the book. While I was still nervous to share this with everyone, I knew it was time. I needed the prayer support to start and finish the book, and to seek God's guidance on what to say. This book was His story – not ours. Again, I received many messages and comments confirming that I should move forward with this book. So, I started writing it.

Chapter 34: God's Perfect Plan

Thursday, April 25 – Tuesday, May 12, 2015

For the next few weeks, we didn't have much to post. We were just working on our "new normal" and looking forward to watching God's Plan unfold. Then, we started to see some of the plan coming to fruition. I had started writing this book, but I hadn't yet mentioned anything about another opportunity to share this story.

Back in January, I had attended the Christian women's retreat, the Soul Spa Sisterhood. Well, my friend was planning the 2nd semester Soul Spa Sisterhood retreat and was looking for a speaker. She asked if I would share this story, and surprisingly, without any hesitation, I agreed. I just knew I was supposed to do this, and God would ensure I was ready.

Since it had been a few weeks since my last post, I tried to put it all into one:

> **May 12th Update:**
> UPDATE: Paul went in yesterday to get his labs. Praise The Lord - the labs all came back improved!
>
> Kidneys:
> Creatinine - down to 1.80 from 2.19 (close to normal of 0.6-1.3)
> BUN - 24, which is NORMAL!!!!!
> GFR - up to 46 from 36. Normal is above 60, but remember it was 8 in the hospital.
>
> Strength - Paul has been back playing basketball 2-3x per week and has golfed the last two weekends. He notices that it takes him a little longer to loosen up than before, but once loose, he feels closer to the way he felt before all of this began.

With our travel, we have had the opportunity to see many people who have been praying for Paul through this entire journey. It is an amazing sight to see him looking so good compared to how sick he was. You can see the tears in many people's eyes as they are sharing their joy for his recovery. It is a truly remarkable story of God's healing power! Truly, we cannot thank everyone enough for all you have done to both pray for healing & strength. We have felt so completely surrounded with love & prayers.

As for me...
The book is coming along. I'm still hoping to have the first draft done by the end of the month. Might end up being the first of June. We will see where that goes...

Soul Spa Sisterhood:
This Friday, I am blessed to have the opportunity to share this story at the Soul Spa Sisterhood Retreat. What a blessing it will be to share God's miraculous work in the healing of Paul! I'm nervous & excited. I am praying God gives me the words to share His Story.

Thank you again for your prayers, love & support!!! Please know we have felt them and we truly know how blessed we are to have each of you in our lives!

Yes! Paul had made it both back onto the basketball court and onto the golf course! While he was still working out the stiffness in his joints, he was able to play both – a true answer to prayer!

I also gave the update both on the book and Soul Spa. I was very excited and nervous to share this story. My friend and I had talked through this a great deal prior to the breakfast. I was thankful for the opportunity to ask for additional prayer support. I knew God would help me through this!

We spent the remainder of the week preparing for the Soul Spa retreat. I prayed that God would give me the words, and the ability to connect to the hearts of the ~50 women who would be in attendance that morning. He knew what parts of the story were important and which parts weren't. He knew what the women needed to hear.

*Please God, please provide me with the
ability to follow Your lead.
This is about You. This is Your story.
Please let them see how amazing You are!*

Friday, May 15, 2015 – Soul Spa Sisterhood Retreat

As I drove to Soul Spa, I turned the radio off and prayed the whole way. For thirty minutes, I sat in silence asking God for direction. And, as I pulled in, a calm came over me. I could feel Him there, supporting me, letting me know I was not alone. He was there with me, and He would provide the words for me.

My friend invited me up, and we sat there for forty-five minutes sharing this story. It was nothing like we planned; it was so much better. She asked questions she wasn't planning on asking, and I shared parts of the story I didn't plan on sharing. You could feel the support of the women in the room. And, as I shared The Gospel through this story, I could see hearts being changed. Some women in that room were Christians, some were seeking, and some were not. While I am not sure if anyone gave their lives to Christ at that time, I do hope that our time together opened the door a little more, so that time for them will come.

After our conversation, we were all given quiet time to pray, meditate, write – whatever we felt called to do. Here was what I wrote:

May 15th – Soul Spa Sisterhood, Collecting God's Miracles:

I was honored today to be asked to speak at the 2nd Soul Spa Sisterhood Retreat, and to share God's story of healing Paul. What is so amazing about the opportunity is that the verse chosen for Soul Spa is:

Mark 6:31 (NIV):
"...Come with Me by yourself to a quiet place and get some rest."

Right after that verse, Jesus performs the miracle of multiplication – feeding 5,000 with five loaves of bread and two fish. But the miracle doesn't stop there. He then asks the disciples to collect the broken pieces – and those broken pieces fill 12 basketfuls!

Here is how it connects – the disciples were collecting that miracle and taking that with them as a reminder of what had just happened. And, I believe we are meant to collect the miracles in our lives – to see them, hold them, and share them with others.

God's healing of Paul is a miracle! There are no other words to describe what God did. It is a miracle. And, I just feel so compelled to share His story – almost like walking through the time of Jesus and seeing the miracles He performed. People couldn't keep it in. He would ask them to not tell anyone, but how could they do that? How could they keep this to themselves? They needed to share it. And, that is exactly how I feel.

I do not know why God chose us for this. I think about the Francesca Battistelli song – **He Knows My Name**. Here is the starting of the song:

"Spent today in a conversation
In the mirror face to face with
Somebody less than perfect
I wouldn't choose me first if
I was looking for a champion
In fact I'd understand if
You picked everyone before me
But that's just not my story

True to who You are
You saw my heart
And made
Something out of nothing."

The blessing is that I get to share God's story of healing Paul. I get to share His words and His healing. I get to share His story. And, truly, I don't feel worthy.

As I shared His story today, I am so thankful He gave me the words to say. He helped me remember the parts of the story that would be impactful to others. He helped me stay strong, even as I was sharing the most difficult times of our life so far.

Heavenly Father,

I praise Your glorious name! I come to You in thanksgiving today for providing Your words and Your strength for the discussion today at Soul Spa. I pray that the women that heard Your story of healing Paul will be able to see both that miracle, and the additional miracles You have provided in their lives.

While the outcome for Paul is nearly complete healing, that is not always Your answer to prayer. We know Your greatness is not tied to an outcome. Your greatness is ALWAYS! You provide miracles each and every day. My prayer today is that we can all see the miracles You provide and share them and Your words with others, so that we can multiply the members of Your church.

Father, I am not sure what You have in store for me next. I pray for peace in the process. I pray for my obedience to Your will and Your plan for me and for our family.

*In Jesus' Name,
Amen*

Afterward

Sunday, August 16, 2015

Well, I am now finished with the first draft of this book. It may not have been by the end of May or by mid-June, but it is now complete. I will send it off to the editor shortly and start the process of publishing it. I am so grateful for the time to write this book as it allowed me to process so many things that have happened – not just in the past several months, but also in the last year.

As for Paul, he continues to heal. He is nearly as strong as he was before this all began. He is back playing basketball a few times each week, and he has enjoyed many golf outings this summer. His kidneys and his joint pain are both improving, but neither are back to "normal". His last few sets of labs showed his kidney function was still outside of the normal range, but it was at least stable. We continue to pray that God will provide the miracle of complete healing for Paul's kidneys.

As a couple, we are committed to our marriage, our family and deepening our relationship with Christ. Like any couple, we have good days and not so good days. That said, we know that, regardless of the events of the day, we love each other and are fully committed to each other. Since March 2nd, Paul still asks me to marry him every morning and I ask him at night. And, yes, it does still put a smile on our faces. And, on the not so good days, it keeps everything in perspective.

The kids are all doing great! Paulie has started 2nd grade and Noah will soon start preschool. While we still have Sarah at home this year, next year she will also be in preschool – how time flies!

They ask questions every now and then about what happened to their Daddy. Paulie asks more questions than the itty bittys, which is not surprising, considering he is the oldest. We pray that, over time, we will be able to share more of this journey with them. We want them to fully see the amazing miracles God provided each and every day in the healing of their Daddy. Their prayers worked. Daddy is home and continues to improve. Praise God!

As for me, I'm still not 100% sure of where God is leading me. I truly feel that, at least some portion of this path will include sharing this story with others. I continue to pray for God's guidance to direct me to where He wants me to be, what He wants for my life. I pray for patience, I pray for peace in this time of unknown, I pray clarity on my next steps, and I pray I will be obedient to that call.

I also have a specific prayer for each one of you reading this story. My prayer is that you saw this story of more than just the *Everyday Miracle* of God healing Paul. I pray you were also able to see how my relationship with God through Jesus Christ allowed me to stay more centered, more focused, more hopeful and more equipped to shine His Light in the midst of the darkest time of my life.

Please know, I write this very humbly. I know that I am not worthy, and only by the blood of Christ do I have the ability to be saved and enter Heaven. Here is an article that has been sent around Facebook several times that does a great job of describing this.

I am a Christian

When I say that "I am a Christian," I am not shouting that "I am clean living." I'm whispering "I was lost, but now I'm found and forgiven."

When I say "I am a Christian," I don't speak of this with pride. I'm confessing that I stumble and need Christ to be my guide.

When I say "I am a Christian," I'm not trying to be strong. I'm professing that I'm weak and need His strength to carry on.

When I say "I am a Christian," I'm not bragging of success. I'm admitting I have failed and need God to clean my mess.

When I say "I am a Christian," I'm not claiming to be perfect. My flaws are far too visible, but God believes I am worth it.

When I say "I am a Christian," I still feel the sting of pain. I have my share of heartaches, so I call upon His name.

When I say "I am a Christian," I'm not holier than thou. I'm just a simple sinner who received God's good grace, somehow!

For years, I sat in the pews of Catholic Churches, listening to the Word of God being spoken. I would feel moved by the service, and then walk out of church and make very poor choices as I discussed in the Introduction.

Even after I accepted Christ as my Lord and Savior, I still spent years "going through the motions". It wasn't until we had trouble with fertility that I made the decision – I needed to be all in. If God would send His Only Son to Earth to die for me, I needed to spend time getting to know Him through His Word in the Bible.

What I had missed for all those years was that God wanted a relationship with me – He wants a relationship with each and every one of us. And, regardless of where we are in that journey of relationship, there are always opportunities to strengthen it.

Some people say that getting into Heaven is complicated. While I am not an expert, I disagree. From what I read, there is one way to get into Heaven – believing that Jesus Christ is the Son of God, sent down from Heaven to die on the cross. He was the last, living, perfect sacrifice – dying for our sins so that we would have the opportunity to enter Heaven. Our price, our ticket to entry, is **full belief**. See, it's not about what we do; it is about what we believe. We could not ever do enough to "earn" our way into Heaven. It's not about works. It is about belief. Here is one of my favorite Bible verses on the topic:

> ***John 3:16-17 (NKJV):***
> *For God so loved the world that He gave His only begotten Son, that whoever believes in Him should not perish but have everlasting life. For God did not send His Son into the world to condemn the world, but that the world through Him might be saved."*

While I don't see this as complex, I also know that it isn't easy.

> ***Matthew 7:13-14 (NKJV):***
> *"Enter by the narrow gate; for wide is the gate and broad is the way that leads to destruction, and there are many who go in by it. Because narrow is the gate and difficult is the way which leads to life, and there are few who find it.*

My prayer for this book is that it inspires each person reading it to take one step closer to Jesus, to deepening and strengthening his / her relationship with Christ and to enter through the narrow gate.

APPENDIX
SONG LIST:

One difficult thing about writing down a list of favorite songs is that, as soon as it is written, another song comes out that deserves to be on this list! I will add songs here that were some of our favorites during this journey. You can always find great Christian music on:

K-LOVE (www.klove.com), Air1 (www.air1.com) and SiriusXM – The Message (www.siriusxm.com/themessage)

Here are some of our favorites (not necessarily in order):

Artist	Song
Matthew West	Day One
	Strong Enough
Unspoken	Good Fight
	Lift My Life Up
	Start a Fire
Casting Crowns	Just Be Held
	Praise You In This Storm
	Thrive
tobyMac	Beyond Me
	Speak Life
MercyMe	Flawless
	Greater
Francesca Battistelli	Free to Be Me
	He Knows My Name

Jamie Grace	Beautiful Day Do Life Big
Sidewalk Prophets	Help Me Find It Live Like That
PJ Anderson	Rise Your Grace Is Amazing
Kari Jobe	I Am Not Alone
AJ Michalka	All I've Ever Needed
Chris Tomlin	I Will Rise
Hawk Nelson	Drops in the Ocean
The Afters	Every Good Thing
Josh Wilson	Fall Apart
KING & COUNTRY	Fix My Eyes
Danny Gokey	Hope in Front of Me
Building 429	Impossible
JJ Weeks Band	Let Them See You
Plumb	Lord I'm Ready Now
Mandisa	Overcomer
Big Daddy Weave	Overwhelmed
Steven Curtis Chapman	Something Beautiful
Tim Timmons	Starts With Me
Newsboys	We Believe